CHALLEN

Ideology, cc

Mi

First published in Great Britain in 2010 by

The Policy Press
University of Bristol
Fourth Floor
Beacon House
Queen's Road
Bristol BS8 1QU
UK
Tel +44 (0)117 331 4054
Fax +44 (0)117 331 4093
e-mail tpp-info@bristol.ac.uk
www.policypress.co.uk

North American office:
The Policy Press
c/o International Specialized Books Services (ISBS)
920 NE 58th Avenue, Suite 300
Portland, OR 97213-3786, USA
Tel +1 503 287 3093
Fax +1 503 280 8832
e-mail info@isbs.com

British Library Cataloguing in Publication Data
A catalogue record for this book is available from the British Library

Library of Congress Cataloging-in-Publication Data
A catalog record for this book has been requested

ISBN 978 1 84742 397 9 paperback
ISBN 978 1 84742 398 6 hardcover

FSC
Mixed Sources
Product group from well-managed
forests and other controlled sources
Cert no. SGS-COC-2482
www.fsc.org
© 1996 Forest Stewardship Council

Cover design by Janna Broadfoot
Front cover: photograph kindly supplied by Getty Images
Printed and bound in Great Britain by TJ International, Padstow.

Contents

Preface

This book originated in a sense of frustration at the absurd proliferation of choices which offer little genuine diversity in consumer markets. My frustration increased as choice was touted as the answer to a variety of policy issues, to which it seemed more a diversion to avoid the issues than a constructive response to them. My perspective was sharpened by reading Barry Schwartz's *The paradox of choice*.[1] Here, I recognised, was a useful input on the problems of choice, but it did not go far enough. Schwartz offers a helpful but mainly psychological assessment of how we experience choice, but does not give full consideration to the social context. This book grew as an attempt to explore matters further.

I am grateful to a number of people for sustaining my conviction that it was a project worth pursuing: to my two elder children Imogen and Cedric for subjecting the draft to the eye of a younger generation; to my friend and colleague Liz Kingdom for a characteristically meticulous review; to Karen Bowler of The Policy Press for, as she put it, being 'optimistic about this one', and engaging with the text in more detail than most editors will do; and to my partner Liz for bearing with my periods of gloom and insisting that there was something worth pursuing. For the limitations of the text which follows, I of course bear full responsibility.

Michael Clarke

Introduction

Go into your favourite supermarket and you will find something like ten thousand different products from which to make your selection. For some this involves bustling round, identifying the necessities for self and family and trying to select the best value for money, or simply the cheapest. For others it is a pleasure to look for new lines and old favourites. The supermarket is but the most prominent example of what is now a leading, if not *the* leading, leisure activity: shopping. Vast shopping centres compete with high streets, department stores with out-of-town megastores, to offer everything from electrical goods through electronics to home furnishings and clothes. Even at home, shopping can continue for many, whether by the now long-established mail-order, or on the internet, where the range of choice is often wider and the prices keener.

Choice and its benefits pervade our lives in other ways. 'Choice', asserted the Prime Minister Tony Blair at the 2005 Labour Party conference, 'is what the rich have always exercised in respect of health and education.' He was determined to make it available to all and it has been a buzzword in policies covering everything from education to social care. As if to confirm him, Jane Fonda told us that, at the age of sixty seven, she needed a hip replacement and, indomitable as ever, she had already selected the prosthesis she would have (and was determined to have the worn out bone dried and polished to adorn her mantelpiece).

As we shall see, however, even supermarket choice is not quite what it seeks to appear, and there are other choices that are more evidently problematic. Some people choose to smoke tobacco, despite its serious health risks. Should they be allowed to continue to do so, particularly in places where their smoke may be inhaled by others? What of the role of an industry that has promoted and sold tobacco for generations and created millions of addicts? Are smokers exercising real choice? Some would defend smokers' rights to continue. Others would argue that, as addicts, they need effective help to give up. Others still would argue (insurers among them) that those who deliberately risk compromising their health – everything from gum disease to heart disease; from impotence to cancer – should not be supported by a health care system funded by those who are reasonably prudent about their health.

And what of the obese, whose numbers continue to rise significantly in the western world, with risks to their health as serious as those from smoking? Surely there can be only one explanation for obesity: overeating, and inadequate exercise to burn off the calories? True, say some, but what you choose to eat also affects the outcome, and some modern processed foods seem to have effects on the body similar to, although not as severe as, tobacco addiction, so that the eater is only ever satisfied for a short time and constantly craves more. Should we penalise or attempt to restrain the obese from their over-indulgence or from their bad choices?

Or does the answer lie in the supermarkets and fast food outlets where their food is sold to them? This touches on a more interesting problem: even if obesity is a rising health problem that promises to be very costly for us all, and even if it is the outcome of straightforward individual indulgence, will it be most effectively tackled by requiring the obese to recognise and fund the costs and consequences? Might it be more effectively addressed by dealing with the food industry, and by exploring ways to mitigate our increasingly sedentary lifestyle?

Choice also manifests itself in even more dramatically fraught situations. Access to abortion has been identified as 'a woman's right to choose'. Whilst some, notably those who regard all abortions as murder, maintain that far too many women have early terminations almost casually, and some that even taking the morning after pill is attempted murder, many others would maintain that the decision to terminate a pregnancy is an agonising one for the woman, but that it may be the best choice for some women in some circumstances.

Equally difficult choices arise when a couple with children separate and one of them forms a new relationship or wants to start a new life that takes them abroad. Should parents be free to choose to follow their passions, even at the price of cutting off the child from the other parent? These and similar decisions involving child custody have no easy, and sometimes no truly satisfactory, outcomes and remind us that some choices are not ones we can opt out of, and may have serious long-term consequences.

These examples illustrate the main themes of this book. We live in a society (and an economy and a polity) in which choice has a central role. It is a core ideology and a major institution. Choice is an idea and a value that is presented as an unmitigated good. Even difficult choices, like those above, are just that, *difficult*, not bad in themselves and therefore to be eliminated as possibilities for choice. More choice, that is a wider range in areas where it already exists, and its introduction where it does not, is always beneficial, desirable and, therefore, legitimising: a matter against which there can be no counter-argument. This is choice as an **ideology**.

Choices also exist in a myriad of different ways as an **institutional mechanism**: in the display aisles, trolleys and checkouts of the supermarket, in the offices, consulting rooms and advice and support systems of the abortion clinic, in the Office of Fair Trading and other agencies designed to secure customers' genuine freedom of choice, and of course in the political system of electoral democracy. All these and many more enable choices to be made in different areas of life, although of course they do so in ways that frame and establish how the choices are to be made. In the supermarket, for example, you select products from the shelf, rather than being served by an assistant, and it is much easier to take what they have, rather than to ask for what you want.

The significance of ideology and its dangers to those subject to it is that it only works successfully if it is not subject to a critical examination. 'Critical' does not necessarily mean debunking hostility. It merely means asking whether things are quite as good as they are made to appear. For the other feature of ideologies is that they serve and reflect interests that are not as benign and selfless as the ideologies are calculated to make them appear.

The ideology and institution of choice are rooted in our (more or less) free market economy and in our political system of electoral democracy. These are fundamental and established institutions tested and developed over several centuries. They have emerged as defensible options as the result of multiple challenges, notably from socialism and communism.

The first part of this book will deal with the very rapid extension of choice in many areas of our lives, and its acceptance as an unmitigated good. It will demonstrate that providing additional choice is by no means always unproblematic or even desirable. This was explored in depth by Schwartz in his book *The paradox of choice* from a psychological perspective, but I will also ask whose interests are really being served: those who are encouraged to exercise choices, or those who provide them.

The second part of the book looks at a different set of choices. These choices can often be important and consequential, and also irreversible. They are diverse, but it will be suggested that the life cycle is a way of comprehending the ways they arise, which they do largely out of the ever greater and more sophisticated knowledge we have of ourselves and the world. These are choices about jobs, careers and training, about partners, children and security, about infirmity and death. These choices are increasingly necessary and new: previous generations did not have to make most of them, or at least far fewer individuals in each generation did. These choices are also difficult: when should I have children? *Should* I have children? Should I live with my partner? Should I leave him or her? Which job should I take or pursue? How should I prepare for retirement? Should I retire at all? Whilst there may be considerable pay-offs for getting these decisions right, there is often no clear path to a good choice and quite often no simply good outcome. These are the demanding and proliferating choices that the ideology of choice as a good does not refer to: hard choices.

The main thesis of the book is therefore that choice and choices, both as a value and as an institution, are ever more abundant, and we are drawn into them ceaselessly, but we need to recognise that not only are they sometimes very demanding and problematic, but quite often they are not nearly as benign as they are presented. Hitler famously remarked that one could never have too much Wagner. Our society is saying the same about choice. I beg to differ on both counts.

This introduction has deliberately started many more hares than could be immediately pursued. Before we can return to the place of choice in modern society, we need to consider what choice is, and how it features and has featured in human life, for the principal point of this book is that choice has a particular salience in the contemporary world, as a value and ideology, and as an institution or range of institutional mechanisms. What we take for granted as normal in the way we live now, in other words, needs to be distinguished into two aspects: on the one hand, the capacity for choice is a characteristic, and, some would say, a defining characteristic, of human beings; on the other, the extent or role of choice in different societies can vary enormously. It is my contention that choice has an exceptionally prominent place in our society, both as a value and as a practice, and some sense of what human beings have been used to is therefore necessary as a prelude to exploring how choice works today.

The next chapter will therefore look at what choice is in the most general terms, and the following one will look, also in general terms, at the way we exercise choice, and the advantages and disadvantages of doing so. This will lead us to review in Chapter Two some of the work done by economists and psychologists on human choice. We can then move in Chapter Three to the substantive consideration of where choice in its modern ideological and institutional form comes from, and the place of choice in a consumer society. This will be followed up in Chapters Four and Five with an extended review of examples of where choice does not work effectively as an institution, and a discussion of alternatives. In Part Two the hard choices now being thrown up by the life cycle – jobs/career, marriage/partnership, fertility/child rearing, retirement/security, and infirmity/death – can be discussed. In conclusion, in Part Three the implications of all that has been discussed for the meaning of our lives and our identities, and how they are sustained, can then be evaluated.

Part One

Choice and consumerism

ONE

What is choice?

How do we characterise choice? Clearly it involves reacting to circumstances, but that immediately raises two issues: on the one hand a deliberate refusal to react is also a choice, and on the other we can think of examples of reaction to circumstances which we would hesitate to call choice. Does the sunflower choose to face the sun? Chemistry would be impossible if different chemicals did not react to one another, but we would not call that choice. This points us to a key feature of choice: mental intermediation. Choices are made by individuals, or sometimes groups, appraising reality, constructing a view of it, and selecting a perceived possibility for action, including refusing to act. The problem with the mental element, however, is that it is at least partially independent from reality.

As so often with concepts, qualities and capacities that we regard as distinctively human, the answer seems to be that human beings have the capacity for choice in a highly developed form, but that other animals also have the capacity in a less developed form. Psychologists have spent much time teaching rats to turn either right or left at the end of a T maze, on the basis that rat learning has similarities to human learning, and it is reasonable to characterise what rats, inquisitive by nature, do at the junction point in the maze as some sort of choice. However, any experimental psychologist will remind you that we are not talking about just any rat. If you put a happy, well-fed rat in a T maze, it may well feel secure, warm and comfortable, and go to sleep. If you ensure that it is hungry, you are more likely to get active choice from the rat. Equally, if you provide a food pellet on the left arm of the maze it is more likely to turn left, and if you provide an electric shock at the end of the left arm it is (after the first time) more likely to turn right. But if you put a Gucci bag at the end of the left arm and a Prada one at the end of the right, the rat will be flummoxed (unless one smells more edible than the other).

The greater the capacity the individual has to recognise and process information, the greater the number and complexity of choices which can be made. Choice involves not just reacting to the world, it involves appraising it – seeing what is there; construing it – deciding how it is organised; making sense of it – putting it in the chooser's context; and identifying a response. As is evident from this, the mental part is often much larger than the crude reality part. Thus, I suddenly feel a sharp pricking sensation in my left leg. I may react with an involuntary flinch and a semi-voluntary exclamation, but my next thoughts are likely to be: have I sat on a pin, or worse, a pair of scissors, or a knife, or have I been bitten or stung by some animal? I probably will not think: has a child crept under my chair and stuck a sharpened knitting needle into me, not because I have looked, but because it is in my experience very unlikely. But if I am allergic to wasp stings, my next move is likely to be cautious, since if it is a wasp and it stings me again I could suffer a life-threatening reaction.

To take a more complex modern example of choice as appraising, constructing and responding, we can look at Nick Leeson, who bankrupted Barings Bank by making unsuccessful trades on the Singapore and other financial markets. Leeson knew what he was doing, although he was much less good at it than he thought he would be. He was able to disguise his failings and continued to draw on more and more of Barings' funds, and commit the bank way over its head, because there was no one in head office in London who understood the derivatives markets in which Leeson was trading. No one therefore verified that he was making the profits he claimed, and no one recognised the extent of the risks that he was running with the bank's money.[1] This example also incidentally suggests a characteristic feature of modern economies. Why was Barings, one of the oldest merchant banks in London, dabbling in derivatives, one of the newest and most complex and risky areas of finance? Because modern markets, especially financial markets, have a huge appetite for novelty: new financial instruments, new ways of trading, new ideas for making money out of money; but this is to get ahead of ourselves. Leeson was making choices that require complex appraisal. He was allowed to continue because head office was content to trust that he understood how best to make those choices.

It is this capacity for recognising and processing information that makes exercising choice such a characteristically human capacity. Other animals can do it, but we can do far more of it. Arguably it has been our capacity to recognise choices and to construct alternative courses of action that has enabled us to become the dominant species. It has also contributed to our capacity for abstraction, for using ideas as ever more complex and sophisticated ways of engaging with reality, to the extent that the ideas themselves become subjects for choices on offer, and have only limited, if any, connection with physical reality, although they may be very influential socially. Thus I may agonise over whether to commit myself to Methodism, and to which variety, or to Episcopalianism, without ever pausing to reflect on whether God exists or not. I may also proclaim my commitment to socialism as a practical political programme of social ideals achieved by social change without having any very clear idea as to where I part company from, for example, social democrats, social reformers, or even from revolutionaries.

As we shall see in later chapters, there are also more practical and no less momentous choices that many people make. Should I have a baby? Should I blow the whistle on my corrupt boss? Should I tell my friend her partner is having an affair? What both these more practical and the more abstract choices remind us is that, for human beings, choices can be hard work. They are not things that are taken lightly, lest they be taken wrongly. They involve a careful investigation and appraisal, a period of mulling over and probably discussion with others, a period of provisional commitment, and then a final decision and action.

By this point someone will be shouting: have you forgotten your supermarket example? Those choices aren't like that at all. Most choices are quick, easy and quite pleasant: 'Tea or coffee sir?' 'Tea please: it's breakfast time, and I always have tea'. Well maybe, but what kind of tea? 'Do you have Earl Grey?' 'No? Then perhaps I should have coffee … but then the coffee is probably worse.' Nonetheless, surely it is the case that most choices are relatively quick and pain free, and a good many are positively pleasurable. Many people love shopping because of the unfettered choices they can make: lots to choose from and few constraints other than what suits you and what is good value for money and, for expensive items, what you can afford. Choosing the annual summer holiday is an extended set of choices for many people, and may be almost as much fun as the holiday itself (and, yes, more so in the cases where the holiday doesn't live up to expectations). Certainly not all choices are anguished, and some are decidedly rewarding. We don't have to make a choice about where to go on holiday or even to go on holiday at all, but I have always fancied Morocco: what do you think?

Some choices are not, or not only, enjoyable in themselves, but empowering. Being able to choose where you live, for example, could have a powerful impact on your quality of life: living space, access to amenities and services, noise levels, congenial neighbours. Understanding the long term value of education in our society, and ensuring that your children understand it and take advantage of it is a notorious source of differential economic success. Working out how to deal with your boss and accommodate his obsession with football and crudely measured productivity at the expense of understanding how to motivate his staff is also the path to making choices that are empowering in themselves and in their consequences.

'You are still making a meal of it,' the complainant will be saying. 'Most choices are much easier than this.' 'Shall we go for a walk? For a drink? Out for a meal? Would you like to read this novel I've just finished? It was excellent, I thought. How many pieces of toast do you want? Would you like some more tea? I'm just going to put the kettle on.' These examples are important and instructive, not because they are less momentous, but because of the fact that they are easy. They are undemanding not just because the issues are trivial, but because the contexts are routinised. How many choices do each of us make daily? Goodness knows, because some are so limited – when do I shift position in my chair, look out of the window, wonder what time it is – that they scarcely get over the threshold of consciousness to count as choices. The vast majority of choices we make are strongly routinised precisely so that we do not have to think about them as full choices. Either they are habits – time to take the dog for a walk – or the context is so routinised that the decision is undemanding.

However, these contexts are different for different people. Thus, if you offered me the novel to read in the example above, it might provoke questioning and a real choice on my part, because I read few novels, but for those who read many it could trigger no more than: 'Oh thanks, I'll put it on my list. I'm reading so-and-so at present.'

As Schwartz points out, routinisation can become more significant if combined with standards:

> We are drawn to people who meet our standards (of intelligence, kindness, character, loyalty, wit) and then we stick with them. We don't make a choice every day about whether to maintain the friendship; we just do.... By using rules, presumptions, standards, and routines to constrain ourselves and limit the decisions we face, we can make life more manageable, which gives us more time to devote ourselves to other people and to the decisions that we can't or don't want to avoid.[2]

We have so far established that, just because choices in the full human sense involve complex appraisal and reflection before selection, choice is demanding. Some choices are very taxing of our intellectual and emotional energies. Even those which are pleasurable processes in themselves can be time-consuming. For this reason most choices are strongly routinised. There are a variety of ways in which we opt out of making choices in the full sense. The most obvious is habit, we do the same as we did in the same circumstances before. Habit and routine govern most of our lives, and enable us to find the time and energy to make real choices. Just how extensive and significant these routines are becomes forcibly evident when they are dramatically interrupted, by illness for example, or by moving house, or by becoming unemployed, by being injured or, most dramatically of all, by being incarcerated.

Beyond the habits we construct for ourselves we rely on others. Many of our routines are governed by convention — for example, journeys to work in most aspects — or by fashion, which governs not only dress and appearance, but modes of speech and topics of conversation.

Beyond this are significant areas in which we could make our own choices, and some of us do, but mostly we rely on the advice of others who have specialist knowledge and skills, often professionals like doctors and accountants, but in practice all sorts of people with specialist skills. Sometimes we turn to friends and acquaintances who may lay claim to more knowledge than they really possess, but who we are relieved to accept as having significantly more knowledge than we do: 'I'd plant aconites if I were you. They always come up a treat in February in a spot like that.'

Then there is the deliberate refusal to make a choice. 'Should I give money to charity A or B? I can't be bothered. I'll do neither.' The same considerations apply to voting in elections. Of course, to refuse to choose is to miss an opportunity which may be advantageous, but as we say to those many cold callers at the door and on the phone, 'we are quite happy to miss the chance of a lifetime today'.

Finally, if we are lazy or bored, we 'pick' rather than choose. Picking involves selecting an option, but not going through the process of appraisal and reasoned decision making, thereby short-circuiting the demanding aspects of choice. The stereotypical example is backing a horse with a blindfold and a pin stuck into the racing column of the newspaper, but we do it in a wide variety of situations. It is the 'whatever' response, the 'I'll have what you're having' decision, and it alerts us to an important aspect of our attitude to choice. Choices are demanding. We do not want to spend all day every day making them in the full sense. Routinising helps, but sometimes we simply want to offload them on to someone else. Significantly, our tolerance of this tactic increases the more exhausted we are. 'What would you like for your birthday?' 'Oh, you decide, it will be a surprise' (and hopefully not of the kind that Auntie Doris's home knitwear provides). 'Where do you want to go on holiday?' 'Oh, you decide.' It also arises in more significant contexts however, and, of course, that is how a lot of babies get made....

Because choice in the full sense is a demanding process we therefore downgrade it and opt out of it much of the time. Filling our lives with that much choice would be overwhelming and disconcerting. We would be considering things we would much sooner take for granted much of the time. It would furthermore make social life very difficult if everyone did the same: interaction would be slow and stilted, rather than as it is, rapid, ritualised and taken for granted much of the time. We are reminded that, although we could do a vast number of things differently, both as individuals and in social groups – be they households, work organisations, or societies – doing things the way they have been done before enables social life to continue. We can concentrate on what we would call the important matters, where we do want to make choices in the full sense. Our habits, routines, conventions and customs sustain a sense of permanence in our lives that is essential to our sense of security, and to our capacity to navigate a way through social relations day to day, and through life. If too many people question too many things simultaneously, anarchy, in the widest sense of a collapse into meaningless chaos, ensues.

The construction of permanence in our lives is a daily preoccupation and achievement. As conscious individuals we are aware that today is unlike yesterday, precisely because we and a large number of others can recall what took place and was done yesterday. Yet today can only make sense in relation to yesterday, and hence must continue and sustain it. Societies vary enormously between one another, and vary much more over time, in the extent to which change is characteristic of them, meaning that yesterday, last month or last year is significantly different from today. Societies with no sense of their own history – where they have come from, and how they got to where they are now – find their very sense of identity and coherence under threat. So it is with individuals in these societies. Thus significant changes take time to bed in, and for those involved to secure themselves again by developing new routines and understandings. Choices need to be worked on to stabilise their meaning and so construct a new secure, routinised world, and restore a sense of permanence.[3]

This is not achieved in isolation, however much it may feel like, and indeed involve, individual effort. To inhabit a secure and apparently permanent world (secure in the sense of sustained meaning and intelligibility, that is, not necessarily financially, or even physically) we require the support of others. Other people need constantly to remind and reassure us that things are as we understand them, and that our routines and expectations are correct. Not just that the number forty two bus to Blenkinsop stops here, but that there is a number forty two bus, and that there are buses, and even that Blenkinsop exists. This reassurance extends upwards into the fine complexities of what different kinds of work are available, and what rewards and pitfalls they have, what marriage and parenthood are, and how to manage them. Anthropologists call this living a constantly acted out set of ideas and practices 'culture'. The more stable, well understood and extensive it is, the more secure and stable (and often boring) the lives of those in the society that sustain it. Societies with weaker cultures, which are less highly integrated, more diverse, with more loose ends and greater rates of change, are hence less secure and more bewildering places to live, with less social support (which does not necessarily mean less goodwill). They are also societies in which many more choices need to be made in a fuller sense: where less is taken for granted. The faster the rate of change, the more demanding this becomes, and the less easy it is to sit back and just let life happen: someone is always insisting we do something new or differently. Sound familiar?

We shall return to these issues again as we deal with others. So far the important points to remember are that:

- real choices are demanding, and for that reason we go to great lengths to routinise them;
- we need a sense of permanence in our relations with others, which we take considerable pains to construct when change threatens it, and for which the support of others is essential;
- rapid changes in societies, and in the social worlds we inhabit within them, force us to make far more choices in the substantial sense than do stable cultures and societies.

There, many choices are foreshadowed, if not foreordained: whom we will marry, or at least a specific indication of the kind of person who is suitable; the work we will do, or at least an explicit indication of the possibilities; how and where we will live, and with what expectations of economic security. Modern industrialised consumer market democracies are not like these traditional societies, and yet for most of human history the world has been much more like traditional societies than our modern ones, and we will explore this further in the next chapter.

TWO

Making choices: just fun?

In this chapter we need to make some preliminary and very general points about the kind of society we live in and the ways in which this interacts with choice.[1] In the next chapter we can go on to look at the more specific ways that choice has become a salient characteristic of our society, and the ways in which it has been presented as a universal good. So, how do we feel about and respond to choices?

Human beings have spent almost all of their existence in conditions in which choices are, in three major ways, limited. First, it is really only in the past century or so, and more strikingly in the past half century, that any societies have moved from chronic economic scarcity to abundance. Even now there are limited societies in which abundance is fairly comprehensive – where it includes services as well as goods, and where it is reasonably widely distributed in society. There are of course almost no societies in which abundance is completely universally distributed, a matter to which we will return in the next chapter. Provision of more than the basic necessities for a substantial majority of the population has enabled a shift from survivalism to discrimination, from coping with the constraints of scarcity to consumerism and its torrent of choices.

Secondly, knowledge about how the world works, both in the grandest and most sophisticated senses – science and technology – and in the practical senses that affect everyday lives, has developed exponentially in the past three generations, and has lain behind the explosion of material abundance. Access to knowledge and a capacity to use it, education, has expanded much more recently, again over the past century, and very rapidly over the past fifty years. This has increased choice in a way that is arguably more powerful and transformative than material abundance. It enables those who have it to recognise the possibilities for choice, to become aware of the choices which are there to be made, and to be increasingly discriminating and sophisticated in making them, whether it be appraising the newly marketed computer game, or evaluating the best way to deal with an illness or disorder, or campaigning for or against nuclear power generation. So great has become the extent, diversity and complexity of knowledge, that in many areas most people are capable of recognising that there is a choice to be made, but also well aware of the limitations of their capacity to make it competently: they may lack adequate knowledge of the topic and/or they may lack the capacity to understand and evaluate it, even if they decide to accumulate the knowledge. In many cases this matters very little. You can still enjoy the new computer game, even if you do not understand its finer points. You can enjoy a new article of clothing in which you cut a dash even if you do not (yet) realise it is made of a material that makes you sweat more.

Finally, modern industrialised democracies are conscious of their relative lack of political constraint. 'It's a free society', we say, implying that no one has a right to prevent you pursuing your course of action. There are of course restraints upon us in every direction, legal, moral and conventional, for example, but relative to the histories of our own societies these are vastly reduced. There are almost no restrictions on how we dress, in our own time at any rate, how and what we eat, where and with whom we choose to live, what work we may do, what religion or political beliefs we espouse, or what recreations we indulge in, except for when there is clear evidence that our activities damage others. Paragliding into your neighbour's greenhouse is not recommended, nor is plotting the elimination of everyone else's freedom of expression by attempting to impose an authoritarian political system.

There are recognised downsides to all these areas of expanded freedom of choice. In respect of material abundance there is the waste that comes from overconsumption and the increasingly transitory sense of meaning that is sustained by goods and services which are discretionary rather than essential. Abundance has generated consumption which is driven by fashion more than need. The problems associated with the explosion of knowledge and the expansion of education have been referred to above. We know and understand a little about a great many things, but very few of us have the energy, insight, or intellectual capacity to understand enough about more than a very few. We even have a term to refer to those exceptional people who do – 'Renaissance man' – a reference to the time, half a millennium ago, when knowledge was sufficiently limited for some people to reasonably aspire to understand it all. This leaves us with enough knowledge and understanding to recognise the choices, but not to feel confident about making many of them. The brittleness of extensive political freedom is evident in a brash individualistic rights consciousness. 'I have a right to use my jet ski.' 'Well yes, but what about the swimmers?' 'I have a right to let the trees in my garden grow to full height.' 'But what about the neighbours' loss of light?' It also manifests itself in a desperate desire to avoid telling people they may not do things, even when their actions may damage others. Tolerance of almost infinitely diverse views and beliefs and only slightly less diverse personal habits and practices is a consequence of this emphasis on lack of political constraint.

Material abundance, expanded knowledge and education, and reduced political and cultural restraints have combined to create vastly increased choice. Few of us would want to return to a past in which these conditions were reversed. There is a very powerful sense that choice is enabling, that it allows us to realise ourselves, to contribute more to our fellow human beings collectively, to make better societies by identifying better ways of doing things. Too many choices, however, tyrannise and overwhelm us. Not all choices are of the variety: which breakfast cereal shall I have this morning? Or even: which new model of television should I buy? Far too many are of the more demanding kind: where shall we go on holiday, and how will we satisfy everyone? Should I buy a house with my lover? Where should we send the children to school? What should be my (or our) pension arrangements? These kinds of choices are more taxing to undertake, more time-consuming and emotionally demanding, less likely to result in a decision about which the chooser is confident, and more likely to entail nasty consequences if they go wrong. They are also not the most difficult of choices we face in our lives – we will come to them in the latter part of this book. Even trivial choices may involve excessive labour: choosing an evening's viewing from two TV channels was relatively easy; choosing from four enabled more discrimination; choosing from hundreds of channels provokes exasperation at the search time involved and about the relative lack of knowledge of some of the newer offerings. You can always get more on TV.

Of course there are individual temperamental differences here. Some people enjoy choosing more than others. Some people find even important choices less stressful than others. All in all, however, the more choices there are to be made, the more time constraining and emotionally demanding they become, and in so doing the more they compete for our energy and other resources, and the less time there is available for getting on with pursuing one selection. In sum, more choice is not an unmitigated good. Too little of it is disabling, too much of it is overwhelming. In this it reflects human character. It is not an abstracted rational process of knowledge accumulation and processing. Minds are not like computers. Choosing requires time for deliberation, which is limited, and requires emotional and moral energy, which is also both limited and consequential in the results of its deployment: how we feel about the choices we have made. That choice is not just fun, even though it can be in some circumstances, should not surprise us. Human beings have survived by combining a developing capacity to use choice to change their environments with a much longer established capacity to survive by adapting to circumstances they cannot (or could not) control. This tendency to respond adaptively has significant consequences for the experience of choice and its outcomes, as we shall see in a moment. For the present we can conclude that choice is distributed in a bell curve in respect of its benefits: too little limits us, too much overwhelms us, hence there must be an optimum point between the two.

This is, however, an abstract generalisation. As has already been pointed out, people vary in their predilection for or aversion to making choices. Like many other social matters, most people also learn to live with making choices, and to enjoy what in the past they may not have, including making more choices. Adaptation is likely in this respect as in others, and we would expect younger generations, who have grown up with more choice, to respond more easily and more positively to it (although not, I will suggest in the next chapter, without difficulty). Nor is there any self-evidently ideal level of choice at a societal level, even if one could determine what might constitute overall levels in a reliably practical way. What can be suggested at an individual level, with obvious implications for the collective, is that increased choice has a paradoxical character. On the one hand, it seems both to increase our actual control of our lives – we can do more to get what we need (assuming we understand what that is), and what we want – and to increase our sense of control, that we are in charge of things rather than being constrained and driven by circumstances. On the other hand, being responsible for maintaining control of so much in our lives increases our sense of liability and, in some circumstances, uncertainty. If we feel confident and have the support of others in our lives, we can make choices and get them right often enough to be able to live with the consequences. If we are isolated and hesitant, we are reluctant to choose, anxious about the consequences and may end up losing out because of missed opportunities, and ultimately being incapacitated by depression. A society with a high level of choices rewards the bold, energetic chooser who researches the choices well, and it penalises those who lack these qualities.

The problems consequent upon choices are hence a burden to be borne by all who participate, although this will be somewhat different for those who opt out. Those who refuse to choose risk missing opportunities that could be to their advantage, and also risk others taking decisions on their behalf, whether at the significant level of others electing a government which acts against their interests or at the trivial level of watching the news when one would rather watch the football.

Opportunity cost, regret and complexity

Besides the general demands of choice referred to above, there are also those of **opportunity cost, regret** and **complexity**. These loom much larger in an environment in which choice is omnipresent, and they are also interlinked.

Opportunity cost is the loss occasioned by pursuing one option rather than another. Thus if I go on holiday to the Seychelles rather than the Maldives, am I risking that by the time I am able to go there they may have been submerged by the next tsunami, or by rises in sea levels? What is for sure is that I shall not be seeing my sister in Sicily this summer, and that means I shall not see my little nephew until he is several months older. Opportunity cost may be substantial: if I stop work to have a baby, will I miss out on the promotion that will enable me to get to senior management by the time I retire, rather than being stuck in the middle levels? As we see here, the greater the opportunities, the greater, inevitably, the potential costs. But life is too short to do everything. Furthermore, doing one thing may also reduce options for doing another later: I enjoy swimming and would love to be a good water polo player, but I know that training for this will increase my weight and I'm determined to be a successful long distance runner.

Opportunity costs are objective but can be very frustrating if, with hindsight, we realise that we made the wrong call. What we feel about this is **regret** – a subjective, but entirely natural, human reaction to opportunity costs: if only I had bought that house when I saw it, instead of putting it off for a year; if only I had taken up the job offer; if only I had responded to that romantic invitation; if only I had stayed at home more and looked after the children. As these examples suggest, it can lead to unproductive 'beating yourself up', loss of self-confidence and can also acquire a moral aspect. Since it is subjective, regret is not inevitable. It is, however, something to which all but the most bumptious of us are prone to some extent, and hence can be counted as part of the increased stresses of pervasive choice. It is a problem exacerbated by individual responsibility for choice, and lessened by the participation of others in the choice. Even utterly shameless decisions, like leaving the children with next door's fourteen year old and going on holiday with the new lover, become acceptable when there are two of you to rationalise and reinforce the choice.

Finally there is **complexity**. In a simple, constrained world of few choices the primary requirement is to persist in doing what is necessary to survive adversities that cannot be controlled. You may nonetheless be knocked back (or knocked out) by other things you understand little and control less, and which you cannot foresee: that is not your responsibility. In a society where almost everything has become your responsibility – how healthy you are, how many children you have, what work you do and whether you succeed at it, who you have as a spouse or partner, let alone *much* more vital matters such as how stylishly you dress, how witty are your comments on the latest film, record or novel, or how discriminating is your choice of home furnishings – the sense of responsibility is awesome if you even dare think about it (most, sensibly, do not), and the result crushing if you cannot keep up the rate of confident and successful choices. Even if you cope with these two problems, it can be mind-boggling in its complexity. It is not just, in other words, the number and sometimes the significant consequences of the choices you need to make, but the interaction between them. It is not just the opportunity cost which means that if you go and see George you will never get away in time to finish off the decorating which you have put off for three weeks already, and Auntie Minnie is coming next week and you need to finish the only spare room. It is that George is in retail finance and you know you need to remortgage and, besides, your husband has said he is really looking forward to a game of tennis with George: 'cont. p94' as *Private Eye* would put it. Such complexities are not confined to the social arena: try engaging in long-term financial planning. It is an excellent idea, applauded by all bank managers and financial advisers, and you know it makes sense, but unless you are prepared to do what they suggest and give them nearly all your income to look after for you, it is almost impossible to get the details to fit together satisfactorily. In part this is because of the complexities of your own financial situation – a personal loan paid off in two years' time, an insurance policy that matures in ten years, a bond in two, your second child going to university hopefully in three years' time, and will your grandfather die? And will he leave you what he said he would? And will your partner's business venture succeed or fail? Complexity derives not just from the interaction of what you know, but also from the vast range of possibilities that can be more or less certain. In the end there are judgements to be made about the perplexities of complexity, but *no rational choices.*

If there are significant and increasing disadvantages to levels of choice which exceed certain thresholds, are there not ways around them? I suggest that there are some, albeit they are not complete solutions. I also suggest that a society which celebrates and seeks to extend choice has also, not surprisingly, produced a number of maladaptive responses which exacerbate the problems of choice. Since choice is a value, as well as a feature of all human societies, and a specific institution in our own, these positive and negative adaptations to choices sometimes have fairly evident evaluative aspects. If we add them up at the end we shall find they amount, on the maladaptive side, to a critique of a choice-ridden society and, on the positive side, to a call for restraint on the unfettered extension of choice. Before exploring them, however, it is worth reiterating the general point made earlier: we have learned to live with choice, and we are all aware that, compared to the not too distant past of a century or so for certain, and some would insist even of half a century ago, our lives are much empowered and enhanced by the choices we have been and are able to make. We have seen, however, that increased choice is not unalloyed good news, and it is the prospects for a future which seems to augur yet more choice that give rise to my initial question: is more choice better?

Adapting to choice: maximisers and satisficers

Herbert Simon long ago noticed that there were two contrasting approaches to choice.[2] Some people are relentless searchers determined not to settle for anything but the best. With the energy they deploy and the skills and knowledge they acquire, many will naturally be successful, at least in comparison to their less persistent counterparts. These he called **maximisers**. They reflect the activities of a consumer market searcher – for the best audio system, the cheapest holiday flight or package, the best offer in the sale, the best deal on a second-hand car, the last thousand pounds off the price of a house. Such people do not also need to be ruthless, still less bullying, just persistent – artful negotiation and the early use of informed contacts may be more successful than trying to batter down the price. Maximising is not confined to the market, however: the complete solution to family squabbles so that everyone is left happy, or the ideal proposal for workplace projects that serves all competing objectives, are also the aims of maximisers. Such people have balancing advantages and disadvantages. They devote more time

---

and effort to securing the result they want, but have the satisfaction in the end of getting it either absolutely right, or as good as it possibly can be. They also strut their stuff in the social marketplace: 'That's a nice car John. How much did you pay for it? Only £7,500: you got a bargain there! Where did you get it from?' This is the cue for an extended account of just how skilful and persistent the purchaser was. Status and social recognition are hence also powerful rewards for the maximiser, who may be approached by others for advice on how to do as well. There may also be considerable satisfaction in the use of knowledge and skills, and in having achieved the best possible result.

The downsides are considerable, however. The process of maximising can very easily become stressful and exhausting, particularly in the latter stages where the obvious avenues have been explored and it is less clear that additional ones will yield real benefits. Nonetheless some temperaments may cope with maximising in a calmer and more measured way than others, though of course if it is a strategy they pursue throughout their lives they will be very busy. The Achilles heel of the maximiser, however, is the inability to settle. Even when you are reasonably confident that you have made the best choice you can, the counterfactual lurks: what if? Opportunity costs also hover around the corner. Would it be better to delay just a little longer to see whether that possibility comes up with something better – a new model, a new store, a new manager, even a new week? Of course some maximisers recognise the hazards here and learn to settle when they judge they have done their best, but both psychology and society (and, it should be said, a good deal of research) are against them. Someone who spends their time persisting for the best outcome will only get there by constantly questioning whether what they have now achieved is good enough. There will be constant examples of outcomes that are better, even if through no failing of the maximiser. It will not be easy to switch off. Further, other people will look to them for results, so giving the maximiser a reputation to maintain. A society in which choice is abundant and celebrated is also a society that celebrates the good chooser. Advertising expects us to seek out a bargain and only settle for the best, to seek the ideal solution. These are matters that need more extensive exploration. It is sufficient to note here that maximising as a style and strategy is supported by a society of abundant choice. One additional element does need to be added here which will be relevant at a number of later points.

Given the status and reputational aspects of maximisers, and their tendency to doubt and regret, the last characteristic that a maximiser would rationally select as a feature of the culture would be competitiveness. Yet modern industrialised democracies are notoriously competitive. The rewards, material and social, are constantly on display, and the possession of those rewards, in education, in work and even more in non-work social life and leisure, in television, films and novels are constantly touted. The maximiser knows then, that, although his or her strategy is not imposed, but a matter of personality and preference, most choices are, to a greater or lesser extent, competitive choices. Either they are part of direct competition with others, or the consequences will contribute to aspects of oneself that are judged competitively by others, for example fashion, lifestyle and leisure choices. In sum, if you are going to be a maximiser, a society of competitive choice would be the one from which, on the one hand, you could expect the greatest rewards and cultural encouragement but, on the other, you would anticipate the greatest stresses and lack of sympathy.

The alternative to the maximiser is the person who operates not by searching for the best available, but according to their own standards in the very broadest sense: they are the **satisficers**. Thus if the satisficer is looking for shoes and sees a pair he likes in the first shop he enters at what seems a reasonable and affordable price, he goes no further and buys them. He is immune to others' comments that they bought a similar pair cheaper elsewhere, or that there is a sale next week at another shoe shop. The satisficer does not seek the best, but what is good enough. Unlike the maximiser, the satisficer is able to settle. This does not mean that she settles for a poor option: standards are standards, and in some matters at least they may be set high, and so require extended effort. The key difference with the satisficer, however, is that she knows when she has got what she wants. She is therefore much less subject to doubt, regret and delay, and much less subject to competitive comparison. Overall the satisficer is much more in control of the process of choice, and much less vulnerable to its open-ended character in many cases, especially in our society.

Reversibility and provision

This leads us to the next pair of alternatives, which again have cultural aspects. Everyone is aware that, in respect of many choices, making the final selection means accepting opportunity costs – you do not want two audio systems, and cannot afford two cars; two jobs, whilst possible, and even necessary for some, are hard to sustain; switching from one to the other may well mean taking a loss, either in cash or in time. Settling is making the choice, but, as we have seen, this may be followed either by acceptance that the choice is final, or doubt, and inclination to revisit it. In some cases a mistake has been made and a revisit may be necessary – the inexact craft of medicine is a familiar example here. In many cases, however, remaining committed to the selection made is the most beneficial option – doctors ask their 'impatients' to give the full course of treatment time to work before looking to another. The temptation is to revisit the choice, and to do so too soon or too repeatedly, especially in our society where choices are abundant. Did you really get the best deal on your credit card, or your gas and electricity, or your phone? It may have taken a lot of searching and quite a while to implement your choice, but if a new offer, which is clearly better the more you inquire about it, comes out in a month's time, it is tempting to give in to the frustration of not having found it before. After all you now know so much more about how to transfer your account. This is the behaviour of the chronic maximiser again, but this time we are looking not at the initial choice but at sticking with it. Is the choice regarded as more or less permanent, or only *pro tem*? One of the most extreme manifestations of this tendency to see all choices as reversible and to avoid commitment is marriage. The grass is notoriously always greener on the other side of the hill, and it is greener just because you can't see that side from where you now are. You may completely accept this point, and agree with your friends that, as the case may be, a roving eye, or an eye for a bargain, may be counterproductive, but you may still be obsessed with the need to find out. This sense of reversibility can ruin holiday plans – does it matter if the Mediterranean is better than the Caribbean; we are

27

in the one and not in the other – and at its extreme can destroy perfectly good marriages.

Revisits to the same choices are not simply all around us, however, they are constantly enjoined upon us. Don't put up with what you have, we are told, seek more, seek better, don't miss out on the new opportunities. Thus we change our homes, our cars, our banks, our solicitors, our doctors, our spouses and even our children on occasions, much more often than we did fifty years ago. There are other reasons beyond choice for this, for example much increased availability, but many choices that were considered more or less stable once made are now seen as reversible. This can only contribute to doubt and uncertainty, at least in respect of those choices that we need subsequently to rely on once made. Further, it deflects us from making the best of our situation and getting the most out of our choices. Commitment leads to investment and exploration of the choice made. If you were not going to trade in your mobile phone after a year or less, perhaps you might explore more of its many functions. The same applies to your husband or wife. Perhaps a mobile phone is a misleading example, however, for each year new models have new and significantly better features: moving pictures, e-mail, internet access. Obsolescence is built into the mobile, as it is built into cars and other consumer goods. This should remind us that even what we may see in others as a personal trait is culturally embedded and supported. We will return to this in the next chapter.

Consideration of consumer durables alongside spouses gives us pause to reflect on how things used to be. Not only was it the case that until the middle of the last century getting rid of your spouse was difficult, legally, socially and morally, commitment itself in that context was less a matter of effort and more a matter of fact. Your marriage and the choice was not reversible, but that did not mean you could not argue about terms and conditions, or the quality of the product. What you wanted, however, was a relationship that worked. It did not in a good many cases, despite the efforts made, which was why divorce laws were relaxed and marriage became a more easily reversible choice.

Some choices by their nature remain irreversible, abortion for example, but in general reversibility has become much more widespread, readily available and expected. Indeed reversibility has almost become a taken for granted feature of choice, so much so that some women will buy clothes on a Friday for the weekend evenings out and then return them on the Monday asking for a refund. Every consumer purchase seems to have its cooling off period and its refund guarantee. The right to choose is not just a one-off right, but a right *cf* to choose repeatedly in respect of the same item of choice. These *Bauman* expectations are now so entrenched that we find it difficult to ask what the alternative is. It is **provision**.

In some areas we still accept provision rather than choice, the reasons for which are interesting in themselves and a matter to which we will return later. Health and safety measures are an example. Passengers on a ship do not expect to be asked what evacuation methods they would prefer in the event of fire, explosion or foundering. They expect effective measures to be agreed, tested and in place, and the crew trained to implement them if need be. Similarly most parents do not want to choose which of the various methods should be used to teach their children to read at school. They want schools to use a method which is known to work, and for teachers to use it competently.

As this example illustrates, provision does not always work. Teachers have been using a variety of methods to teach reading for the past half century, often with firm convictions but with deplorably inadequate results. However, parents would not necessarily have been better off having a choice about which methods were used, because they did not know which one was best either. Nobody did. The point is that all parents want their children to be taught to read as early as is reasonable for the child and expect all schools to be able to provide that. Provision is at present lamentable, with twenty per cent or more going into secondary school unable to read at an appropriate level.[3] In the past a great deal of social and economic life was founded on provision not choice, not always with beneficial outcomes. Those who can recall the days when telephones were provided, after an inordinate delay, by the GPO, now BT, would agree that provision does not always work. The point, however, is that an alternative to choice exists, and that it functions on a quite different basis.

—

Provision requires that standards of performance that are agreed as adequate be met. The supplier does not have to be a monopoly. Medicine is an obvious example, where patient choice is possible between and within local GP practices, but the same standards of competence and performance are expected of all doctors. There is a tendency to uniformity in provision, however, and to a limitation on choice, and hence a focus upon providing goods or services to a clear set of standards with little emphasis on customer selection, and little incentive to differentiation. Societies based on provision tend to be paternalistic or authoritarian – the state knows best – where societies based on choice are market driven – the consumer (or is it the market?) knows best. These are issues to which we will return in the next chapter, but for the present it should be noted that extending choice indefinitely is not the only possibility.

There are implications with quite important consequences when considering the alternatives of provision and choice. Choice places the responsibility for the choice and its outcome with the chooser. This is a necessary consequence of the choice itself. If the chooser were not responsible for the choice, he could not really be said to have made that choice, since whoever was responsible would be waiting in the background. This is in fact how we teach children to choose at times. Sometimes we stand behind them to rescue them when they make the wrong choice, and at other times we let them suffer the consequences of making a bad choice, in order to learn its lessons. This is also how we attempt to avoid responsibility for choices: something or someone else 'made me do it' or 'misled me'. Adults, however, are usually liable for their choices, although, as we shall see, it has been difficult to sustain the old-established principle of *caveat emptor* – let the buyer beware – fully in many contemporary choices.

The alternative position, where provision is substituted for choice, is that the provider has the obligation to care for the experience of the receiver. Customer care is hence an obligation. The point of customers is that your obligations to them are limited, as of course they discover rapidly when they have recourse to customer care departments, which exist to fend off rather than deal with complaints. Where care is being explicitly provided, but the recipient is designated a 'customer' this produces an absurd conception. Care of the elderly,

for example, can only be 'care' if the carer is permitted t
to the receiver and minister to his or her needs as identifi
expressed. If the carer is restricted to, for example, only cle
only providing meals, only assisting to dress or undress, or (.o
any combination of specified tasks, 'care' is impossible. Care is not
to be confused with provision, which may be of a limited product
or service, but to agreed standards. Care goes beyond standards in
an open-ended way. It is the opposite of as well as an alternative to
choice in this respect, since what the carer is providing is not specified
or bounded. Care shares the paternalism of provision but, besides
having no detailed limits, explicitly allows for interaction about what
is provided between the two parties on a continuing basis.

Individual and collective choice

We have seen in this chapter that choice involves responsibility for
it on the part of the chooser. It is worth adding that in our society
responsibility is almost entirely individual.[4] This is one of the features
of life that we largely take for granted, but choices can be collective,
as they sometimes are with couples and with families, and often are
with institutions, such as schools, hospitals, churches, sports clubs
and businesses. Who gets to participate in these choices, even though
they bind everyone, is widely variable, but important consequences
flow from collective and socially supported choices, that is, those
where others are *consulted*, even if they are not parties to the choice.
Individual choices emphasise the autonomy of the individual, and
many expressive choices in respect of leisure and lifestyle, for example,
are intended to do this. Collective and socially supported choices
are much less exposed and much easier to defend and sustain, and
hence less vulnerable to regret, doubt and reversibility. This does
not mean that collectivities, whether couples or businesses, do not
make mistakes, or make choices they regret. Anyone who has lived
in either knows that they do. It means that the resources available if
doubt arises are much greater, not simply because the involvement
of, say, two people doubles the capacity to reappraise the situation,
but because of the social and emotional support that two or more
people can provide one another: 'yes, we made a mistake and we are

—
31

responsible, but anyone could have done it and we are not idiots'. Note that recourse to individualisation – 'it was all down to Jones in marketing, he dreamt up the idea' – treats the choice as an individual one, not a collective one. The extent to which individuals rather than collectivities are the unit of choice in society will, then, influence the way choices are experienced. On the one hand we have the possibility that all choice is collectivised, and no one makes decisions without collaborating with others, and on the other a society in which many, if not most, choices are made by individuals, and responsibility even for many collective choices is seen to lie with individuals. Formally we can locate choices in the individual even, for example, by assent or dissent in committees but, in practical reality, committees and much else that is social are sustained by collaboration, conformity and acceptance. Only by having regard for others are sustained social relations possible. It is therefore significant that there could be no society in which all choices were individual; it would be anarchy in the strict sense of the term.

Making choices more or less stressful

We have then two sets of circumstances in which to envision choices being made and people making them. One set reduces the stresses of choice, the other sustains, and in some respects enhances, those anxieties. The **satisficing** chooser acts in relation to standards and settles without difficulty, whereas their **maximising** counterpart finds it hard to settle and is beset by the problems of **opportunity cost** and **regret**. These problems are exacerbated by seeing choices as reversible, rather than as a commitment to be made the best of, as a result of which the best may then be got out of them. Individualised choice and responsibility for it in a culture emphasising the right to choose in respect of everything burdens people with the liability for their choices, whereas a society characterised more by **provision**, with the responsibilities it leaves with the provider to maintain adequate standards, lessens the burden on the individual. Leaving space for care to sustain some relationships, leaving them open rather than formally or functionally defined, further softens social life. By contrast, making competition a leading feature of culture and the basis for reward in economy and society increases the pressure that choices bring. Choices taken with social support or collectively also spread the load and provide room for protection and support when choices are difficult, and when they go wrong. These points do not quite add up to an account of contemporary industrialised democracies and the place of choice in them, but they do illustrate some significant features, such as the links between choice, individualism and competition for example.

This chapter has stuck largely to the individual and social psychological level, because we tend to see choices as individual matters, and because wide-ranging accounts of changes in the economy, polity and society are easier to grasp and evaluate if they can be related to their individual impact. Before moving to an account of a society which celebrates choice as a central feature, moral and practical, it is worth noting a few more problems with the way in which choice works at the individual level, problems which will be further illuminated by the account of society which follows.

Adaptation: a sting in the tail

First let us return to our characterisation of human beings as, on the one hand, succeeding by adapting to conditions they cannot alter and, on the other, planning and considering ways to change their own circumstances. I suggested that, although today we see the latter as the norm, and all problems − individual, group, social or planetary − as to be identified, engaged with and overcome, our history has been based on the former. For most of our existence we have had to struggle with conditions that we could not alter and which we understood very poorly. Being good at putting up with difficulty, adversity and loss has had a psychologically beneficial effect. It is not simply that we did not let cold, hunger and disease get us down, but that we accepted them for what they were for us: part of normality, albeit at times an unpleasant normality. We adapted to circumstances that were often difficult and always, apart from for a very few privileged people in good times, limited. We developed a default mode which was accepting, which was just as well, since we would otherwise have probably died of frustration. This, however,

—

has not proved such a successful tactic in a society of abundance, in which it is constantly open to us to strive for more and more rewards, and in which the physical risks of cold, hunger, disease and insecurity are largely taken care of. When we achieve these rewards – a pay rise, a new car, a new relationship – they do indeed buoy us up no end for a while, but after a quite limited time we adapt and normalise them. This is bad news in various ways: the pay rise will give me more money in my pocket, and it will help sustain my sense of value in the world, but getting the next one, at least in short order, will require even more effort. Whilst there is no limit to the number of pay rises I could theoretically get, there are limits to the number of people who are going to go on getting them. The new car will not remain new, and will rapidly become a not so new one which looks much less appealing as more friends and colleagues acquire newer ones. And the new love? It doesn't bear thinking about in this connection does it, but we all know what is possible. The rudest thing you can say of someone in the exciting world of choice is that they have become 'boring'.

This process is well documented by psychologists, who refer to it as hedonic adaptation.[5] Rather nastier is its offspring, the satisfaction treadmill. This describes the way in which, if we make a series of successful choices, we can get our satisfaction levels nicely raised, so that life is distinctly pleasurable. The difficulty is that we adapt quite rapidly to the newly achieved pleasurable circumstances, and when we reapply ourselves to restore our level of satisfaction we find we have to do more than we did last time to achieve the same results. We are becoming used to success itself.

One of the difficulties here is that the goalposts for achievement are always moving. More is constantly expected – a greater work rate, a new set of consumer durables, a new lifestyle, a new home. Whilst we may be trying to achieve some of these goods for practical reasons – most people have central heating now, and children do not get chilblains in the winter for example – much is also coloured by fashion and status. Fashion makes us want to discard things that are perfectly serviceable, but *so last year*; status pushes us to obtain things which may be social, such as membership of exclusive clubs, as well as material. Both fashion and status are competitive and rely on the notion of being up there, ahead of the crowd and select. Whilst anyone with either the fashion sense or the money and the right advice can be fashionable, status is hierarchical and exclusive by definition. As its external appearances are mimicked it moves on, except in certain respects. Some things are by definition in short supply – status conferring honorary positions for example, such as membership of the Royal Society – and others are in short supply physically – nice houses by the sea for example. When we compete for these *positional goods*, as Hirsch aptly called them,[6] as we must if we are to have them, our choices are increasingly constrained. We are constantly looking over our shoulders and become snappish and brittle when confronted socially with the limitations of our achievements. Choices in connection with status striving are fraught with increasingly fierce competition and diminishing returns. Of course none of us would admit to it for that very reason, until, that is, we hear that the Joneses have acquired such a pretty country cottage, or that the Smiths have a seriously tasty new car.

Although taking as its starting point the argument that some significant degree of choice is much better than very limited choice, this chapter has identified some of the ways in which an abundance of choice is less than wonderful news for us all. We now need to return to the matter with which we started, that is, the recognition that choice has dramatically increased in recent generations. It is time to ask how and why this has happened, in order to get a grip on why it has such a central role in our lives.

THREE

Choice and the consumer society

There will be those who will have responded with frustration to the last chapter: 'This is all about process, not outcome. So we have a lot more choices to make than we used to, but we have adapted, we cope with it. You pointed out that adaptation is what we are good at. Maybe choice is not always fun, but overall its expansion has given us a vastly increased control over our lives, individually and collectively, and enabled us to do things undreamed of in the past. It is the results of the expansion of choices we should be looking at, the benefits of societies with extensive choice.'

The main claim of this book is not that choice does not and has not conferred benefits, but that it is by no means the universal boon that it is usually assumed to be, and that its unlimited further expansion cannot be assumed to be *ipso facto* beneficial. The last chapter laid the groundwork for understanding how choice works at an individual level. This is a theme that will be completed in the latter part of the book, when we look at choices and the life cycle. In order for that to be set in the necessary social context, however, we need an understanding of the kind of society that has come to celebrate choice as a great good. That is the object of this chapter. How and why did choice become so widespread, and to be seen so positively? Does it really deliver what it claims? (This chapter does not pretend to provide more than a standard account of the development of industrial society, with an emphasis on the emergence of consumerism. Sociological sophisticates may therefore want to move quickly to the latter part, or on to Chapter Four.[1])

The societies which today have choice as their central feature can be identified by their leading organisational characteristics. These in turn remind us not only of how society is organised today and why, but of how we got here. The characteristics also have *values* associated with them, which justify, express and celebrate the way in which these societies work. The key characteristics are science, industrialism, capitalism, democracy, their offspring social democracy, and its offspring mass consumption. The associated values are knowledge, freedom, choice, individualism, competition, tolerance and progress.[2]

Industrialisation and the acceptance of constant change

Industrial mass production, the use of machines to produce identical goods in quantity, provided the basis, for the first time in human history, for the elimination of scarcity. It did not achieve this in a generation, but the application of machines, first powered by water, then transformed by steam power and finally refined by the introduction of electricity to tasks which had up till then been done by hand, produced changes in society from which we are still reeling.[3] Industrial mass production made possible the output of not only far greater amounts of goods than craftsmen could achieve, but in many cases the uniformity that machines could provide also improved quality. The invention of machines also meant that the tools of the craftsmen's trades and the craftsmen themselves became progressively redundant. Whereas in the past output depended upon the skills taught, usually over an extended period of apprenticeship, formal or informal, and maintained by the esprit de corps of the workers themselves, organised in some cases into guilds which exercised powerful controls on methods, standards and prices, machines now occupied a central place. The machine worker's skill lay in ensuring the machine worked as it was supposed to, and in maintaining it, which rapidly became the job of a new set of workers – the engineers who produced and maintained the machines.[4]

The significance of this change lay not just in the shift in the balance of power between men and machines, and in the vastly increased productivity of machines, mightily consequential in themselves, but in the prospect of innovation which would continue indefinitely. Machines were constantly improved, became faster and more precise, and machines were introduced to perform jobs which had so far been difficult to mechanise. Some areas of the economy were mechanised much earlier than others. Thus, for example, cotton production was transformed by the application of steam power and increasingly sophisticated machines to spinning and to weaving looms. Printing, created by the invention of type and then movable type in the fifteenth century, was transformed by the application of steam power in the nineteenth, permitting the development of mass circulation daily papers and mass circulation books. Construction, by contrast, has proved much harder to mechanise, and is still dominated by craftsmen: bricklayers, carpenters, electricians, plumbers, glaziers, albeit the introduction of steel and concrete and a degree of prefabrication and sophisticated lifting gear has made a big impact in the last half century. The constant development of technology has hence not just destroyed the old crafts, with their stable hold on vital production processes, but has generated a cascade of new jobs, both more and less skilled. So, for example, the shipwrights who managed and constructed Britain's merchant and naval ships using wood, and techniques progressively refined over the centuries, were superseded in a generation or two in the nineteenth century by on the one hand naval architects and engineers like Isambard Kingdom Brunel, who designed the first iron ship, the *SS Great Britain*, and on the other by riveters who secured the metal plates with an entirely new technology. Riveters were in turn superseded by welders in the twentieth century. On board ships, sail makers, carpenters and shipwrights were replaced by engineers as wood and sail were replaced by steel and steam, and then by petroleum.

The changes produced an economy, and a society based upon it, in which change is seen as inevitable, continuous and beneficial. Production constantly becomes larger in scale, more efficient and cheaper per unit of output, but this is only achieved by constant technical innovation, which in turn means that no occupation is secure. The background to the industrial revolution lay in the increased understanding of the physical world, which was achieved by the rapid development of science in the sixteenth, seventeenth and eighteenth centuries. The emergence of physics, chemistry and biology as distinctive sciences with increasingly powerful and wide-ranging bodies of knowledge, proven by repeated and increasingly precise experiment, gave human beings a capacity to manipulate the world that had no limits to its development. This contrasted with the history of societies up to this point, which were constrained by limited knowledge and constantly aware of their vulnerability to famines, disease, war and other disasters. These were societies of scarcity, constantly struggling to produce enough to survive, and to defend themselves against encroachment by others. Their inclinations were hence *conservative*: maintain the tried and tested ways of doing things that have enabled us to survive in the past. Challenge these and all may be lost. Change was viewed with caution, because change was associated not with something done in a new and more effective way, but with change suddenly imposed by forces beyond your control, and with results equally uncontrollable. The very name of the Conservative Party indicates its attitude to change; and it is the oldest party, the renamed Tory Party, the tradition representative of the landowning classes, the opponents of the Whigs, who represented the manufacturers (among others). Fear of change was also very evident in the period leading up to the civil war, and was one important reason for the restoration of the monarchy.[5] It was also evident in the reluctance to enact electoral reform in the early nineteenth century – the period leading up to the 1832 Act.[6] Industrialisation, based on the application of science in the development of an unending cascade of new technology, transformed the idea of change into something that can be controlled for the better, and increasingly projected human beings as the masters of, rather than the subordinates and victims of, physical and social reality. Change came to be seen not as threatening, but as progressive.[7] In 1851, when Britain staged its Great Exhibition, confidence in the first industrialised society was high that man was now well on the way to being in charge of nature and that, whilst an endless list of difficulties remained to be addressed, we now had the means to do so, and we should continue to press forward with industrial development with optimism and enthusiasm.

The political consequences of industrialisation

We have concentrated so far on the economic side of the industrial revolution, but it also had political and social consequences. The political order of preindustrial societies was based on the need for security which, it was broadly accepted, could only be achieved through relying on what had succeeded in the past. That meant both an economy and a division of labour which changed slowly, if at all (though it did change substantially in the centuries preceding the industrial revolution), and a political system based equally on caution, which in practice meant deference to established hierarchies. Those who, as families, had demonstrated their capacity for the exercise of power and the acquisition of wealth that usually went with it in the past were accepted as the leading candidates for power and control. Individuals might succeed or disgrace themselves, and societies might be based on monarchy or aristocracy, and a new star might arise from relative obscurity to establish a new family by dint of energy and ability and the capacity to form crucial friendships and alliances. There might be a greater or lesser degree of popular participation in government, limited in practice to the tier below the ruling elite, whether these were the full citizens of the slave dependent societies of Greece and Rome, or the small landowners and burghers of the serf and peasant dependent societies of medieval Europe. Democracy existed as an idea, but its practice was limited, both in terms of who had democratic rights, including an electoral vote at all, and in the acceptance that aristocracies were not available for electoral elimination as ruling groups, even though actual rulers and lesser power holders could be forced out or assassinated if they were seen to fail to deliver.[8]

The industrial revolution introduced a political transformation in several respects. In the first place it developed a new basis for acquiring wealth and, although the landowning aristocracy participated and many saw their wealth increase, for the first time they had competitors. Landowners were able to take advantage of their land by developing transport routes over it by canal, road and rail, by exploiting its mineral resources, notably coal, iron and other metals, and by benefiting from increased land values in areas where the new industries generated new cities, and from the new wealth of larger administrative centres. The industrialists, those who undertook the innovations and risks of the new economy (hence the term entrepreneur, derived from the French verb *entreprendre*, meaning to undertake), largely came from more humble origins, however.[9] The challenge they posed was twofold. First, they offered the prospect that, if they could sustain their ingenuity and energy, they could not merely become wealthy, but go on getting wealthier indefinitely, while the prospects for the landowners were more limited. Land could be exploited for minerals, transport and building, and agriculture could be, and was, made much more productive, but the balance of advantage in the longer term lay with the industrialists. Secondly, the industrialists benefited from the changes they introduced, and hence were firmly in favour of the right to continual innovation, and increasingly convinced of the beneficial consequences for the economy as a whole in the medium and long term.

Crucially the new industrialists tied the right to invest their money or capital as they chose, and the right to enjoy the benefits or suffer the adverse consequences if they made mistakes, with political rights. The industrial capitalists argued that the benefit of industrial production was so great, both actually and above all potentially, that economic decisions should be unconstrained. If a manufacturer backed an innovation which did not work he would lose money, and perhaps go bankrupt. If he produced goods no one wanted he would also fail. Only the market should therefore decide what would succeed and what would fail. In contrast, in the managed markets of the preindustrialised societies the idea of the amount of goods and services of different kinds needed and available was understood, and the cost of their production was reflected in the idea of a fair price and a just wage for the time, costs, skill and effort of their production. Exploitation of market shortages, both of goods and labour, was legally and administratively limited. Industrial capitalism now insisted on a move to an open, unconstrained, free market, where demand for goods and services alone would determine success or failure.[10]

At the same time the manufacturers insisted on their political right to participate in the running of society. A good many were elected as MPs, and unsurprisingly the sentiment of this new group of wealth creators was in favour of the rights of all to participate in the new system, and antagonistic to the continuing predominance of those born into privilege, wealth and power. At the same time the industrialists, organised in time into a political party to press their case and their aspirations, were by no means in favour of the unfettered extension of democracy. After all, the mass of the people were still, as they always had been, poor and ignorant, and largely seen as incapable of making a serious, that is to say informed and reasoned, contribution to political life. The key test was the market. If you could participate in markets that were unconstrained by rules banning newcomers and privileging established interests, then market participants would, by their choices, determine your fate. If you produced what was wanted, or needed, or what appealed, and it was of an adequate quality, you would prosper. If not you would fail. The great strength of the industrial capitalist argument lay in demonstration: look where we have come from; our system works.

Markets and their problems

This, however, introduces us to the problems that arose with industrial market capitalism. Markets are competitive, which is their virtue: excellence is rewarded and privileges and established positions are not respected; but at the same time their vice: failures are not market abstractions but involve human beings. If it were simply venturesome entrepreneurs who failed in the marketplace, no doubt many would have said that this was no more than the rough justice of the market. Industrial production may be driven by innovators and entrepreneurs, but it is actually implemented by those they employ. This group was always vastly greater than the numbers of industrialists, and has become progressively greater, because constant innovation has led to progressively vaster machinery for production. The early iron works founded by Abraham Darby in Coalbrookdale could be fitted into a large back garden and run by a dozen or so workers. A modern steelworks occupies a square mile or more and employs thousands of workers. Employees have always been essential to industrial capitalism, despite its constant emphasis upon investment in new machinery and the undoubted effectiveness of machinery in producing more at reducing costs. Employees hence became the dependent, neglected element in the capitalist equation.

Employees were vulnerable in three persistent ways. First, if the industrialist got his planning and investment wrong, and was either beaten by the competition, or produced goods or services which were not much in demand, he would fail, and hence his employees would be redundant. Secondly, if he succeeded, the process of innovation itself requires constant re-equipping, reorganisation and retraining of work forces. Skills become redundant, and workforce numbers may fall as machines can do jobs for which workers' hands and brains were previously required. Further, success by the entrepreneur may involve takeover or merger with competitors in the marketplace, which involves the rationalisation of production facilities and administrative staff. All are the basis for employees to lose their jobs, and potentially to find their skills irrelevant in the marketplace, like those of the riveters in the shipping industry, or more recently of coal miners.

All of this might be argued by its defenders to be a necessary feature of the new economic order, to be made good by the success of the economy as a whole, and hence its capacity to create new employment to replace the old. Although it should be said that the transition between the two may well be a lot smoother for the economists and politicians who proclaim its virtues than for those actually experiencing it. The third weakness of the new industrial capitalism, however, offered no such even theoretically easy transition. From quite early on industrial production showed an alarming tendency to catastrophic collapse, at least in part because of its very success.

Markets rely for their effective working upon a willingness of people with money to buy goods and services in them. There are a variety of reasons why people may be reluctant to do this, despite the attractions of the marketplace in normal circumstances. Markets may become saturated with goods. This happened with the cotton industry, one of the bases of industrialisation in the first half of the nineteenth century in Britain. People were glad to be able to buy cotton goods of improving quality at lower prices. An initial virtuous cycle took place. As prices fell more people could afford more cotton goods, which sustained profits and investment, and so supplies increased and prices fell further, all of this at the same time providing employment and stimulating competition to develop ever more efficient and innovative production machinery. In the end, however, everyone had enough cotton goods, and buying slowed. Even distress pricing, selling at below cost, could not sustain demand. The entire system collapsed upon itself. People did not buy, so many factories could not produce, so workers were laid off and factories closed, so in turn more people had less money and less purchasing power. A virtuous cycle turned into a vicious slump until eventually people's cottons wore out, and they became increasingly desperate for new ones and the cycle started again.

Overproduction is a persistent source of the business cycle in industrial capitalist economies, to which consumerism is the contemporary solution, a matter to which we will come below. There are other reasons for a collapse in demand, however. Loss of confidence in the currency through gross inflation is one, general economic insecurity and hence a propensity to save rather than spend money is another. Violent external events such as wars, political crises and the sudden rise in the price of a vital economic resource such as petroleum can all have a shock effect on economies, which are in the end composed of people making choices and who, in such circumstances, become significantly more reluctant to venture into the marketplace. This does not involve some kind of panic hibernation. A significant blow to market confidence that merely reduces willingness to spend can initiate a downward spiral of falling prices, failure to attract custom, redundancies, loss of spending power and business failures. Historically these processes happen in cycles of boom and slump, which at times have combined with other circumstances, and with poor decision making by governments attempting to manage the economy, to result in prolonged depressions.

Engaging with the problems: socialism and social democracy

The reaction to this substantial downside by the great majority of economic participants – employees – was initial acceptance of it, and then organised resistance. This resistance took on an additional sharpness as it was recognised that the new industrial economy had another nasty anomaly. Although industrial mass production generated, as we saw above, enough, and at times more than enough, for all, and, at least in good times and perhaps in the long run (in which, as Keynes remarked, we are all dead[11]), increased living standards for all, the benefits of the new economic system, were distributed very unevenly. True, wages would go up in times of boom, but they could disappear altogether in times of slump. The real beneficiaries were the new wealthy industrialists and those with the money to invest in backing them financially. The mass of the population hence remained poor. This had historically been seen as inevitable. In an economy rooted in scarcity and survival, poverty was regarded as natural. It was mitigated by charity, by the obligation to try as far as possible to ensure that there was work for all, and by the notion of a fair wage. The free market system had no such provisos. Where poverty in the midst of persistent insecurity and scarcity was seen as inevitable – 'the poor are always with us' – in an economy of ever increasing wealth and abundance it could not be justified. These defects in the market based industrial economy, capitalism, had to be remedied, and there were two strategies on offer, the socialist and the social democratic.

Both these alternatives offered to use the state to remedy the ills of the new capitalist market based economy, the differences between them lying in the extent of intervention. Socialism envisaged complete management of the economy in the interests of all. Thus it accepted the advantages of industrial mass production and constant technological innovation, but sought to eliminate what it saw as its irrationalities by centralised state planning and management. Individual and social need, implemented by planning, would hence be substituted in economic analysis and in government for market demand, and markets would be regulated to ensure supply. Ownership of industrial enterprises would be collectivised. Different variants of socialism opted for different political systems – a political party to lead and control things, or workers' control of enterprises; egalitarian or less egalitarian distributions of wealth and income; participatory or representative democracy; and the achievement of socialism by incremental or revolutionary expropriation of industrial and financial proprietors for example. The aspiration of socialism was, however, the ownership of the economy by all citizens, and hence the participation of all in its management and its benefits. Virulent and at times fratricidal debate raged as to the best detailed variant, but the key question remained whether markets and demand in them would be the arbiter of success, or whether organised planning and management of supply and demand would see a more effective and much more just solution. There was a clear intuitive advantage to the socialist alternative. Since the industrial revolution was itself the outcome of the application of dispassionate technical knowledge born of experiment, it surely followed that collecting as much knowledge as possible about the working of the economy and its various markets, and its exploration to create rational economic planning, was only the application of scientific principles to the new economy. Rationally informed policy choices were better than leaving matters to be dealt with by the uncontrolled consequences of a myriad of decision makers in the markets.

Socialism as a set of values and as a political and economic aspiration has not died out – Socialist parties still exist – but as a set of practical proposals it has never succeeded. It failed most spectacularly in the areas of its greatest success: in the state socialist economies of what, following the Russian revolution, became the USSR, and then the Soviet bloc. The Soviet Union collapsed at the end of the 1980s under the progressive weight of its cumbersome economic, administrative and political machinery in the face of long, determined competition with the 'western bloc', dominated by America.

The social democratic alternative has by contrast been, in one form or another, almost universally successful. Its aspiration was not to substitute comprehensive ownership of enterprises and control of markets, but to leave ownership largely in private hands, and progressively to mitigate the damage that free market capitalism brought. This has been achieved by selective degrees of intervention to control markets, and by the increasingly comprehensive imposition of limits, standards and guarantees by regulation. Thus, some markets are under more or less comprehensive state ownership and management: defence, health and education for example, in Britain at least. Others are subject to considerable intervention: gas, electricity,

—

47

water, telecommunications and aviation for example. Still others are subject to a lesser degree of regulation: most of the manufacturing and retail industries for example, although employees, customers and the public at large are now extensively protected by health and safety and environmental regulation, and by compulsory warranties and compensation guarantees on many goods and services. Rather than taking over enterprises and markets, the social democratic strategy has been to regulate and manage them at arm's length, to manage private advantage flexibly in relation to the common interest, and to avoid the catastrophes to which markets are prone.

This process is bolstered at central government level by macro-economic management: control of the money supply, changes in interest rates to regulate the cost of borrowing, schemes to promote and support training, support for new industries, support for research and development and in trade negotiations with other nations, and many other tactics. At the same time the worst effects of the inegalitarian results of the market economy are mitigated by direct state intervention through progressive taxation. Not only does the state take money from almost everyone in order to redistribute it, for reasons of efficiency and social justice, but it takes more from those who have more. Thus taxation is used to provide basic incomes for those who have none, and to provide essential services for those who either cannot afford them, notably housing, or for more or less everyone on the basis that comprehensive provision is both the fairest and most efficient solution, health and education being the leading examples in both cases, with options for private sector choice if individuals so wish. The extent of intervention, taxation and provision varies between political parties and from country to country, for example Scandinavia has one of the stronger versions of the social democratic solution, America one of the weaker. The point is that all successfully industrialised societies have been forced to mitigate the problems of market failure and inequality under the pure market system by variants of social democracy. In so doing industrial market democracies have been able to test the claim that industrial production linked with markets as arbiters, rather than comprehensive state control, can in the long run, and sometimes in the not so long run, raise living standards for everyone.

—

In this they have succeeded dramatically. Poverty has not been eliminated, but it has been reduced to proportions unimaginable a century ago, save in the most rosy socialist vision. Economic and social security has been created as a powerful political expectation that drives every government from election to election. It lies behind the aphorism that opposition parties do not win elections, governments lose them. They do so by failing to deliver economic success and security. With the eclipse of radical socialism, and notably of its communist state socialist version as a reference point, politics has increasingly converged into a technical debate about how best to manage the economy, and how most fairly and effectively to share out its benefits among the population. Paradoxically, and despite their rhetoric, the final drive to success against the Soviet bloc in the 1980s by the vociferously pro-market leaders of the western economies, Ronald Reagan and Margaret Thatcher, did not involve the destruction of the social democratic project, but rather its entrenchment. Much was said of rolling back the state, freeing markets from restraint, reducing welfare and other state benefits and privatising state-owned industries, and it is true that the tax burdens on the rich were lessened, state intervention in some markets was weakened for a time, and employment in the Civil Service stopped growing quite so rapidly. The powers and capacities of organised labour were cut back, but in the end these leaders and their parties faced re-election, and that could only be achieved by delivering an economic success that could be felt by the vast majority: even leaving out a significant minority risked resentment exploding into violence, as it did in British cities in the 1980s' riots.[12]

The inevitability of social democracy

The social democratic project was hence not just a possible response to the downside of industrial capitalism, it became a strategy essential to its survival. Although born of adversity in the nineteenth century, it became increasingly seen as critical to economic success in the twentieth century. All those poor, ignorant, unhealthy people with their high birth rates and short lifespans were increasingly seen not just as unfairly treated, but as economically inefficient, particularly as international competition increased.[13] That competition found its most decisive expression in two world wars, where it was recognised that the winning side would not be the one with the best generals, or the best trained armed forces (important though those were), but the side with the greatest sustained productive capacity, the capacity to produce more and better armaments systems, and the infrastructure to deploy and support them. Maintaining a population which was poor, ignorant and unhealthy was not economically sensible. Hence educating, housing, training and maintaining the health of the entire population became both socially just and economically essential. To put the issue the other way round, the higher standards became for the better off, the greater the cost of merely subsidising those who, for one reason or another, could not contribute significantly to the economy. Making sure that everyone contributes to the maximum extent of their natural abilities to their own and others' benefit hence became an economic goal which reinforced a sense of social justice.

Although this objective was formalised in the early years of the twentieth century by social democratic parties, and crucial steps were taken to establish the basis of the welfare state in Europe in the early years of the century, and in America in the New Deal response to the depression of the 1930s, it was only after the Second World War that real determination was shown to provide full employment, universal health care, housing and education, and the extension of social rights of citizenship.[14] The postwar boom, which lasted until the beginning of the 1970s, owed a good deal to widespread acceptance by most political parties and by electorates of the social democratic project, labelled subsequently 'the postwar settlement' in Britain. This enabled the social democratic project to deliver in terms of increasingly widespread rises in living standards and the introduction of comprehensive state services in housing, health and education. The more educated and well-off proved, not surprisingly, to be more effective consumers of state services, but an increasingly large majority of the population benefited substantially and over the longer term.

The rise of affluence and the new Right

Industrialised democracies remain, in essence, based on private ownership of business, and on free markets, however. Competition remains an important driver. The rich continue, as they always have, to get richer, even though the poor have become rather less absolutely poor – most have the necessities for survival.[15] An increasing middle group of beneficiaries came to dominate the stage, the affluent, those whose work and prospects were improved by the spread of health care and education, and by the rapid expansion of the service sector of the economy at the expense of the manufacturing sector. There were many casualties as the new far-right politicians of the 1980s attacked the 'sclerotic features' of the social democratic project as they saw them, notably the restraining influence of organised labour, and they happily presided over the demise of long-established manufacturing industries – coal, steel making, shipbuilding – and the ruthless internationalising of others, some painfully, as with car making, others ebulliently, as with banking and financial services.

These nasty episodes reminded the population that the economy remained based on market competition. If governments smitten with social democratic wisdom or aspirations did not intervene, nasty episodes and much unpleasantness were still likely, as British governments discovered to their cost as they struggled with an unruly workforce prone to strikes, official and unofficial, and to increasingly aggressive marches, demonstrations, picketing and factory occupations. By the 1980s however, the zealously pro-market politicians were well aware that they were constrained by their own need for re-election, and for that they had to deliver benefits to the great majority of the electorate. They were also aware that, by this stage, the social democratic project was increasingly taken for granted in its achievements. Much as they wanted to revert to an early nineteenth century position of minimal state intervention and to allowing markets to generate their own solutions, in the belief that intervention was only a form of state socialism (which did not work), there were at least three powerful reasons why they could not. In the first place economic arguments had become quite persuasively added to social justice ones in favour of the social democratic project, as indicated above. Secondly, the benefits of the economic security which it offered had been enjoyed by increasing numbers for too long for them to be put at risk without considerable political cost. Finally and most intriguingly, there was a paradoxical consequence to the spread of economic security. Although people would obviously be fearful of losing the economic security they had, a question arose of what was the next objective. The social democratic project made powerful sense in terms of social justice, and in terms of economic competitiveness. If most of the population was now healthy, housed, educated and affluent, however, and operating at present levels of workload and economic efficiency would keep them there, what was the point of pursuing even greater affluence?

Of course there are negative arguments. Competition, both local, from the individual standpoint, and international, from the nation's, could be argued to consign those who fail to continue to compete, innovate and be more productive, not to lack of growth, but to failure and economic decline. This was the argument, but it was increasingly belied by counter examples. Britain had grown far more weakly than its competitors in the postwar years, and yet affluence and the social democratic project had succeeded. As the rhetoric and action of the new Right became more ferocious, societies with their own social democratic achievements in Europe began to look askance at the insistence on market responsiveness, change, more work and the necessity of growth; France and Germany, notable exemplars of successful postwar reconstruction based on hard work and state intervention, firmly begged to differ. Maybe their living standards were no longer going up much, and maybe unemployment was becoming more of a problem, but this was no catastrophe, and perhaps preferable to the frenetic Anglo-American alternative.

The coming of affluence

By this point, however, the crucial changes had already largely taken place: the shift from a mass production to a mass *consumption* society, and to an economy driven by wants rather than by needs. This process did not begin in the 1980s, but in the midst of the drive to achieve the social democratic project in the 1950s. In 1959, as Harold Macmillan led the Conservative Party to another victory with the slogan that 'many of [the population] have never had it so good',[16] he could claim in support of that not only unemployment levels below one per cent and rising real incomes, but a massive and sustained effort at the clearance of unfit housing (or slums) and its replacement by a mix of state and private housing, with the prospect that unfit housing would soon be eliminated. Galbraith was writing about the 'affluent society'.[17] A few years later Goldthorpe and Lockwood were beginning their detailed studies of Luton, as a basis for examining what affluence meant at the grass roots.[18]

Affluence meant mass economic security and the possibility of incomes remaining high enough to buy more than the absolute necessities of life. At least in the modern industries in Luton, Goldthorpe and Lockwood found that high wages, often sustained by regular overtime, were the basis of a transformation in working-class communities. The neighbourliness, with its elements of mutual support in what was usually chronic economic adversity, which had characterised vast tracts of industrialised cities since the nineteenth century, and given rise to distinctive institutions – pubs, football clubs, chapels and churches, working men's clubs, choirs and bands, friendly societies, trade union branches, for example – had not been recreated in the new town of Luton. It was replaced by a more inward looking, family based, economically orientated existence. Workers devoted their energies to acquiring the equipment for a secure and comfortable life: cars, telephones, washing machines, fridges and home ownership.

Were these affluent workers therefore now middle class? That was an issue that increasingly mattered little. They did not see themselves as middle class. Their quest for home comforts was not also a quest for higher social status. It was the failure of the Labour Party to recognise the significance of these changes, and a dogged pursuit of the full realisation of the social democratic project in the 1960s and 1970s, that led to the party's near collapse in the 1980s. True, in the 1960s there was a long way to go to provide real universal access to decent standards of living for all – that is still not achieved in the twenty first century. The Labour Party, however, clung for too long to a belief that organised labour, articulating ideas rooted in earlier periods of strident class struggle, could be the route to ultimate success. This set up a paradigm of struggle over the control of the economy in a quasi-Marxist sense: employers would seek to extract as much profit as possible and to make workers work as hard as possible; employees must organise through trades unions to force wages up and resist unreasonable working practices, and elect trade union sponsored governments, in order to increase taxes, especially on the rich, so as to provide state benefits for all, and a degree of equality. This resulted in an increasingly sour conflict between unions and employers, with a Labour government desperately trying to hold the ring, and being constantly humiliated.

The new Right, led by Margaret Thatcher, was portrayed as the party of the rich, and engaged in a programme of tax cutting and of creating the opportunities for business that undoubtedly made a large number of well placed people rich. The government's top priority was the destruction of trade union power, which it achieved decisively by restrictive labour legislation controlling industrial action, by gladly allowing industries suffering from severe international competition – coal, steel, shipbuilding – to collapse and their workforces, often in single-industry towns like Corby and Consett, to become unemployed, and by engaging in a set-piece struggle with the most militant union – the mine workers – achieving a comprehensive victory followed by the rapid closure of pits.

Surely such a government could not succeed? Even if a jaded electorate gave it a chance once, it would not repeat a mistake that was going back on the social democratic project? Labour sentiment would surely be galvanised and the rising unemployment levels and the destruction of industries would produce a decisive swing back to the established path. True, Labour sentiment *was* galvanised, but around its traditional class rhetoric. The electoral results were disastrous. What the Conservatives had recognised was that by the 1980s affluence had spread far enough to form a centre of political and economic gravity. It was not Luton that was taken as the epitome of the new order, but Essex, with its brash money motivated individualism, and Essex man became the Thatcherite totem. If you persuaded Essex man that he could do well, and provided good opportunities to make money for himself by his own efforts and ingenuity, not necessarily in employment in a large plant, but in self-employment, being adaptable, perhaps being willing to move to another town, or a new job, then he would vote Conservative. Incentives were provided to encourage people to see themselves in a new classless and economically independent, money orientated light. Council homes were required to be sold to sitting tenants at large discounts, vastly increasing the numbers of homeowners in a few years and, in doing so, symbolically destroying the visible legacy of the social democratic project. The houses that Harold Macmillan had been so proud of providing to the poor, whose pitiful conditions had first led him into politics in the 1920s, were now privatised, no longer the responsibility of a paternalistic (and latterly, it should be said, often neglectful) state. State enterprises were privatised in a double blow to traditional Labour ideology. The aspiration to control the economy outlined in clause four of the Labour Party constitution sought state ownership of the commanding heights of the economy. It had been put into effect dramatically with the nationalisation of coal, steel, railways, gas, electricity, water, air travel, ports, buses and some road haulage under the 1945 Labour government. All were now sold off and the proceeds devoted to tax cuts and government expenditure. At the same time the very process of privatisation itself was rigged. The share offerings were deliberately set up to ensure that the market price when trading in them began would be above the sale price set by the government, so that all investors would make an immediate profit. This was coupled with large advertising campaigns encouraging citizens who had never before invested in the stock market to do so, and guaranteeing that they would receive a minimum allocation of shares, as well as with restrictions designed to prevent the wealthy from making a huge killing by buying up large numbers (restrictions which were often ignored and evaded by the rich).

Finally, the increased mobility of labour which was encouraged as a vital means to ensuring that the economy remained flexible, dynamic and competitive meant that occupational pensions became difficult to sustain. At the same time, rising incomes meant that the state pension, one of the earliest elements of the social democratic project, initiated by one of the last Liberal governments, before the First World War, was increasingly expensive to maintain. The government switched it from keeping pace with earnings to keeping pace with inflation, and encouraged everyone who did not have the prospect of an occupational pension to take out a private pension and save regularly, providing a range of incentives to do so, and running another huge advertising campaign to encourage people to get started.

The importance of these changes is that they recognised the success of the social democratic project. Despite the Conservative government's anti-state, anti-socialist, anti-welfare rhetoric, it did very little to dismantle what had been achieved. State housing provision continued for those who needed it, though increasingly through specialist housing association charities funded by central (not local) government. Health and education remained state services, despite tinkering and more rhetoric. Welfare benefits became less generous, but remained in place, and ironically remained a major demand on government expenditure as a consequence of ruthless pressure to drive down inflation and a refusal to support uncompetitive industries, both of which drove up unemployment levels, in some areas for long periods. The size of the state itself was not reduced, even if its growth rate was slowed. The poor certainly suffered more, and the rich benefited more under the new Right, but neither group was electorally decisive. It was the affluent middle income group that had to be wooed, and it was not until the Labour opposition fully accepted this and abandoned its class rhetoric that it defeated a Conservative government which had by then long run out of ideas, practical political energy and economic competence.

The legacy of the new Right: the consumer society

The significance of the new Right in the 1980s and 1990s lies in its capacity to recognise the direction of change, and to be seen to be capitalising on its advantages, and in so doing cementing it into place. The changes to 'privatised economic instrumentalism', and moves away from solidary collectivism which the Luton studies had identified, were epitomised in Thatcher's assertion that 'there is no such thing as society, only families and individuals'.[19] Her policies deliberately sustained this move to individualism – the property owning democracy, owning and responsible for their own houses and buying and selling them in a sometimes volatile marketplace, rather than having them provided for rent by the state; the share owning democracy seeking greater risks in the equity markets, and no longer dependent on the building society on the high street; and individual responsibility for long-term financial security through a private pension, rather than relying on the state. The latter two were much less successful than the first, with most buyers of state privatisation shares not retaining them for long, and private pensions proving a long term fiasco (to which we will return). The point, however, is that the shift in values and beliefs towards a more enthusiastic embrace of the market, with all its risks, was successfully promoted at the expense of established social democratic state provision.

At the same time the economy continued to grow, not as fast or as evenly as in the long postwar boom, but it grew, and it has grown since. That growth has made us all richer, albeit the benefits have continued to be very unevenly distributed. Further, the structural changes in the economy away from manufacturing and towards the service sector, and the increasing rate of change in the marketplace as a result of the impact of information technology and greater flexibility in working practices, work organisations' responses to new markets, and takeovers and mergers created an environment in which, besides more frequent job changes and shifts in career direction for most, there was an increasing homogenisation of work around a white collar mode, and away from a bipolar blue collar–white collar mode.[20] This new environment, in which change is endemic, inevitably brings with it a lack of rootedness – people no longer expect to work for one employer, with one set of skills, in one industry all their lives, as many used to. At the same time, because of relatively high employment levels (though not as high as those of the 1950s) there are expectations of reasonable economic security and rising real incomes, as the economy continues to grow (most commentators on the current economic situation agree that the setbacks of the recession and credit crunch from 2008 are not expected to change this pattern permanently).

It is this combination of circumstances that has brought the consumer society to fruition. Affluence for the majority is now taken for granted; it is just a question of degree of affluence: whether you

—

live in a £100,000 house or £1 million house, whether you drive a five year old Toyota or a new BMW, whether you holiday in the Costa del Sol or the Caribbean, whether you read the tabloid *Daily Mail* or the tabloid *Times*. In either case you will follow football, play golf, have children who go to university, think about remortgaging, enjoy drinking wine and going out to eat, have a daughter who is mad on horse riding whose achievements you film on a camcorder, and whose tendency, real or imagined, to indulge in sex, drugs and junk food you worry about.

This society is centred around the family, still highly significant as a social, emotional and economic reference point, despite its fracturing over the past half century with the rise of divorce, the decline of marriage and the growth of households with step-parents and step-siblings, but above all it is centred on the individual. Such are anticipated rates of social and economic change now that the one thing that children know as they grow up is that their lives will not be like those of their parents save in one respect: expectations that one way or another their incomes will be sustained, and will grow. They do not expect to have the same or similar jobs as their parents, perhaps not to have domestic lives like their parents, though they are more likely to expect the explicit struggle for domestic success to be repeated for them, where their parents experienced the contrast with their parents, who kept their domestic problems out of public view to maintain social respectability. What they do expect, however, is a continuation of the wide ranging and unending series of choices with which they have grown up, and to which their parents have had to adapt.

The politics of consumerist choice

The shared characteristic of all, or almost all, of these choices is that, although they are variously consequential, they are not permanent, and in most cases are reversible. They are also individual. 'Should I buy the latest personal audio system?' Yes, but in the expectation that a new and better one will arrive before long. 'Should I buy this car or scooter?' Yes, but in the expectation that it will last only a limited time, and that if it does not suit it can be traded in for something else.

'Should I buy this house, even if it is beyond my means?' Yes, because its value will go up, and it can be sold if you get really overextended. 'Should I take this job?' Why not, if it appeals? You can leave at any time without disgrace, and you may be restructured, downsized, or outsourced by that time anyway. 'Should I buy a house with this man or woman?' Why not? The relationship might work, but if it does not you can sell up and move on. 'Should I go on an expensive foreign trip which I cannot afford on savings?' Why not borrow on the equity of your flat and do it anyway?

This perhaps presents people in an unfairly insouciant, even cynical, light. I am not suggesting that people consciously take serious decisions lightly, but rather that the circumstances in which they take them have been changing. Choice in the reversible, inconsequential version of it has become pervasive. With the achievement of the social democratic project, politics has become evacuated of values other than practical economic ones. Parties all agree on an enduring obligation to social justice, the social democratic obligation to continue to reduce poverty, and to provide certain state services on a universal basis, but the real action is around competence in economic management and arguments about sharing out the benefits. Thus political debate has become centred on small increases in growth, inflation and unemployment, or penny changes in tax rates, and above all upon conveying an impression of competence in managing the economy. Voters are then encouraged to opt for whom they have the greatest confidence in the process of constant careful trimming: sustaining corporate profits and stock markets, but avoiding speculative booms, keeping house prices rising steadily and neither crashing nor exploding, keeping inflation positive but limited, keeping unemployment and interest rates within five per cent, keeping incomes rising gently but steadily.

The benefits of a consumer society are hence enormous freedom of choice, a lack of constraint politically, culturally and economically. The rules of the social and economic game have changed. No longer will you work in the same industry that your father worked in; neither any longer will the job you first seek to apply yourself to and acquire skills in sustain you throughout your life; but if you apply yourself, constantly take opportunities as they arise, are willing to change jobs

—

and not be deterred when you lose them, there is plenty of money to be made. You will not live in or near the town you grew up in, not just because of the attractiveness of moving elsewhere socially, culturally and economically, but because the town you grow up in will not remain the same, but be transformed by new building, new industries, new transport systems and a new population. But the rewards of moving from place to place, between countries and continents, as well as regions, and in the course of one job as well as from one job to another can be exciting and rewarding as well as challenging if you are willing to engage and not look back. Similarly you cannot rely on your first serious domestic relationship surviving, even if it results in children. There is no avoiding the anguish of its failure if that happens, but if you can move on emotionally you may well succeed at your second or subsequent attempt in establishing something more durable.

This is a society in which choices are on the one hand constantly required, and on the other constantly offered, a society in which the active chooser is the one who survives best, by seeking out, recognising and taking opportunities, but also one in which indulgent choices are part of reasonable expectations: 'Do I feel like a pizza or an Indian?' 'Fancy a break in Prague? Or Tenerife?' You cannot have whatever you want, but most things you can aspire to, if not this month then next, if not this year then in a few years' time.

Credit and consumerism

These aspirations can be brought much closer to realisation for the individual as a result of the development of an institution central to the continued growth of consumer society: credit. The first credit cards were introduced in the 1950s, when they joined hire purchase for expensive consumer goods. Unsecured personal loans arrived in the 1960s, and mortgage lending was vastly extended and diversified in the 1980s, culminating in the almost instant mortgage loan, coupled with easy early equity release. The outcome has been a steady rise in borrowing, both secured and unsecured, fuelled in recent years by a more aggressively competitive credit industry eager to corner yet more of the money you have not yet earned.[21] The great advantage of this development for the consumer economy is that, by encouraging people to borrow what they cannot presently afford, they shift their perspective from coveting a new item to concern that they keep up the repayments. Struggling to earn enough to do this then fuels a feeling of more entitlement to indulgent spending – 'I've worked hard, so I'm entitled to a reward' – and so to the purchase of the next item on credit. The vital thing is never to look back and evaluate the benefits of what has been purchased: what did we really get out of that? Do we really *need* what we're talking about buying? The answer to all these questions is almost invariably 'no', at least in any very sustainable sense of 'need'.

The Achilles heel of consumer society lies in its superseding of the social democratic project. That was concerned with providing for everybody's needs. The more the social democratic project has become entrenched and successful, the more it is taken for granted, and a new agenda anticipated. The new Right attempted to identify that agenda with restraint on further and fuller implementation of the social democratic project and a shift to market based individual self-reliance. It was forced to accept in time that the social democratic project would remain in place, and that continuing to fund it would be a sustained and intractable concern. Nevertheless, the spread of affluence and its explosive expansion through credit did enable a shift to individualistic market orientated values to take place. The rapid growth of consumer choice sustained a brash individualistic rights consciousness: 'I can do what I want, and my money is as good as yours'. The downside risk of job insecurity and constant change was accepted as the cost of this. It could only be maintained, however, on the premises, first, of continued delivery of the services of the social democratic project and, secondly, of continued practical success in macro-economic management to sustain economic growth and relatively full employment.

What must not be allowed to happen, however, is for the workforce to stop and reflect on what it does want, and how much effort it is prepared to put in to pay for it. Credit subtly avoids that arising by claiming that the new things can be had immediately and paid for more or less painlessly in the future. In times of high inflation and steadily rising incomes this is an attractive strategy: the real cost of what has been bought is eroded by inflation, and earnings rise to make repayments increasingly trivial. Such is the experience of the few who remain in homes bought on their first mortgages. As time passes and the cost of housing increases, and with them the size of new mortgages, the repayments on one needed fifteen years ago become smaller by comparison. In reality, however, the length of time mortgages are maintained has declined to not much more than five years, and the temptation is to renew them at the same term, twenty to twenty five years, to minimise the payments. At one time older borrowers were increasingly inhibited from doing this by lenders insisting loans be repaid by retirement age, but now such considerations are being abandoned, and interest only mortgages are widely available, where the loan is never paid off and the lender inherits the property on death, with the family getting such equity as is then left.

From the macro-economic point of view, maintaining workers/consumers/debtors on the treadmill is vital. Consumer economies are sustained by consumer expenditure and consumer confidence. The entire operation is like an Indian rope trick. Everyone has to maintain confidence and commitment to borrow more and earn more to pay for what they are induced to want, with advertising, marketing and branding as front-line tactics to keep consumers wanting things. If consumer confidence starts to falter, willingness to continue to borrow and spend, not the same as they did last year, but more, will come into question, and the demand for goods and services will slacken, putting more people out of work and leading to a downward spiral of recession. Hence it is vital that nobody – or at least no credible group of people – stand up and say: 'Wait a minute, what's the point? Why do we need all this?'

Consumerism and the emperor's new clothes

Criticisms are easy to make. Why are consumer durables not durable, but built to fail in a quite limited time? Why are so many things not worth repairing? Why is so much that is bought subsequently thrown away well before it has become unfit for service: last year's clothes, last week's food, the last generation of personal computers or audio systems. Built-in obsolescence – they don't make the parts for it any more – has long been with us. The change has gradually come in the nature of the benefits. Televisions used to be unreliable, with grainy pictures in black and white. They became more reliable, acquired colour and improved definition, and larger screens. A string of further refinements continues to take place, but the incremental value of them is less. We are tempted, as with so many other goods and services, with bells and whistles, the increasingly vast array of additional functions and gadgets, and by progressive reductions in price.

The significance of this process, however, is less in the trivialisation of the refinements offered than in their contribution to making choices indulgent and inconsequential: what you fancy rather than what you need. Fashion and lifestyle feeds into this, and reminds us that the consumer society is not only individualistic but competitive and market based. People are not merely encouraged to engage with work markets and to earn more, but to compete with others in an environment that explicitly aims to reward the wily, the clever, the persistent and the skilled. If the social justice element of the social democratic project has succeeded in giving everyone equal access to resources and engaging in the work markets – a claim that is a good deal truer now than it was half a century ago, although still far from entirely achieved even if widely asserted – success means success as a *person*, being a better person than others, and spending the income that results shows others how far you have succeeded. Buying that new fitted kitchen with the up-to-the-minute work surface and the equipment in the latest style is important, even if you never cook and usually eat out.

Conspicuous consumption – showing off your wealth – has been a feature of many societies, including our own, for centuries. Its varieties and pretensions have often been derided. That does not make it any the more appealing today, but that is not the greatest of its drawbacks. It is today part of something greater. Status striving through competitive consumption is an aspect of consumer society which celebrates choice as a central value. 'Getting and spending', as the Victorians called it, for status reasons is a way of justifying a continuing flow of choices which, through being made, validate themselves, because status conferring, and validate the chooser as

—

having thereby made good choices and acquired, or more likely confirmed, a certain status. Because consumption is now so broadly spread, it is less rigidly bound to semi-formal class status, and more concerned with the construction of individual identity: just as I am a teacher, I am also a yachtsman and a lifeboat supporter, a Christian and a folk music enthusiast.

In a society of growing abundance, but where not all needs are met, which was addressed by social democracy, choices are not only restricted by circumstances, even if progressively less so than in earlier history, but the main choices, from which many others flow, are relatively self-evident. As consumer society succeeds social democracy, which as we have seen is a gradual and overlapping process, choices become discretionary. For a time status can take on a substitute role: the choices are still self-evident, not because of economic necessity, but because of status driven social necessity. As status considerations have declined, however, and even golf clubs struggle to find more members, rather than to exclude the socially unacceptable, consumption choices become purely personal. The price of that, however, is that their meaning is also purely personal. When membership of the golf club meant that you had arrived socially, playing golf had a meaning that was powerfully socially supported. When it becomes just a recreation (unless you are a professional), it is just a question of the pleasure you derive from honing your physical skills and from talking to others doing likewise, though the social world of the nineteenth hole may remain for some. In a full blown consumer society individualism is extended to an extreme degree, and choice continually shades into hedonism: 'want' is less socially structured and more personal. Choice is free, but increasingly confusing: how do you sustain the meaningfulness of choices? Does it matter if you do not, since nearly all are reversible? How do you avoid a manic progress from one option to the next, never finally settling on anything? How in the end do you know what you do want to do, other than, as the rather cynical modern phrase has it: it seemed like a good thing at the time?

Tolerance as a leading value of consumerism

The descent into this dizzying void of meaninglessness is made no easier by the corollary value that accompanies the spread of individualistic choice. If you are to be allowed to make free choices, the obvious constraint is how they impinge upon others. In the past these constraints have been socially very proximate. A combination of legal, financial, conventional and status limitations restricted not only what you could do that impacted directly on others, but also what you could do even if you kept it segregated. Thus it was only two or three generations or so ago that women were largely socially excluded from pubs, and that taking off your clothes on the beach was illegal everywhere. The price of increased individualism is *tolerance*: we conclude that we should accept what others do and think, even if we find it uncongenial or even downright immoral, unless we can show that it is clearly damaging to others who do not willingly collaborate in it. This tolerance has its origins in the Reformation that permitted more freedom of thought in matters of religion, and which in turn sustained freedom of thought in inquiries into matters philosophical, scientific and political, so permitting the development of science and the drive to democracy: those who came to have a right to think for themselves came to expect the right to express their political views in an electoral vote. Whilst tolerance may have a collaborative side, it can also end up segregating. Tolerance for the views or practices of others may engender curiosity, greater understanding and greater respect for difference. It may also result in careful social distance, and indifference to others, provided that they keep to the rules sustaining tolerance and avoid impinging negatively upon you.

The impact of increasing diversity was commented on long ago, by writers during the industrial revolution who were concerned at the moral disintegration of society involved, and who wondered where it would end. Emile Durkheim was a leading writer in this vein in respect of France at the turn of the twentieth century, for example.[22] Diversity and tolerance has advanced very considerably since then, and we may reasonably point out that, despite two world wars, France and Britain have prospered and not fallen apart, either as economies or as societies. Nonetheless tolerance has now proceeded to the point that it is almost the only value, along with choice, that commands universal agreement.

Choice, tolerance and meaning

We have reached a paradoxical point. Choice has been elevated to a central value of the consumer society, necessarily so, since if workers, as consumers, do not keep choosing and spending, the economy will stop. Yet the meaning and value of the choices made is increasingly less self-evident, because they are less tied to *need* and more to *want*. Want, in turn, is less tightly organised as society has become less class and status bound. Choices are hence more individualistic and, for that very reason, less easy to sustain in terms of their meaning. Choice is also very powerfully sustained as a value because markets are based on choice and it is the market economy that has produced the abundance of the consumer society. Further, choice is enabling, because it allows people to engage with the world and improve their lot in it, and the more knowledge and freedom of action they have, the more, and more effective, choices they can make. The same values are deeply entrenched through the notion of freedom of political expression in electoral choice. Finally, choice can be fun; it can be doing what you want. Choice has hence become something that cannot be criticised, that is bound to be beneficial, no matter how much further extended, but which is becoming increasingly individual, and in becoming increasingly individual is also becoming increasingly meaningless and transitory. The outcome is a society dedicated to constant effort to produce more in order to be able to consume more to increasingly less purpose.

Because choice has become a powerful value underpinning consumer society, and justified in depth by the historical development of society, it is increasingly difficult to perceive its downsides. The descent into individualistic confusion and sometimes hedonistic mania is one set of problems. There are specific circumstances where more choice is counterproductive, however, some of which we will now turn to, as well as to a series of extremely problematic situations in the life cycle, to which aspects of the consumer society that have not been at the centre of discussion in this chapter have given rise.

—

FOUR

When choice does not work

The last chapter looked analytically and historically at how a society dominated by choice – a consumer society – developed, and where it came from. This chapter provides a range of examples of how that society and, in particular, choice mechanisms work; or, rather, examples of how they work inadequately or perversely. By using examples it does not seek to be exhaustive, or to condemn the consumer society as comprehensively pernicious, but rather to indicate some of its limitations which, as it has been argued throughout, is a matter that choice as an ideology naturally ignores.

There is a very wide range of circumstances in which choice produces adverse rather than benign social consequences. We have already seen in Chapter Two how this can happen at an individual level, but at a social level the problems arise more from the outcomes of using choice where it should not be, or where it should be constrained. Sometimes, as we shall see, these consequences are an outcome of choice as an institution – choice as the mechanism for deciding what happens rather than some other means – and sometimes the adverse consequences are the result of the power of choice as an ideology – people are encouraged to take liberties. Sometimes the impact of choice is plainly evident in negative outcomes, notably where it is inappropriately used in markets, and sometimes the impact is on culture, where some may regret changes in a way of life now more influenced by choice, and others may not, perhaps because they have been so influenced. This reminds us of a point made earlier: attitudes to choice vary very considerably between individuals. Some people welcome choice despite its complexities and risks (on which see more below), while others may find it burdensome.

Does choice overwhelm or empower?

Simply stated this is the first example of the socially problematic nature of choice: it may overwhelm rather than enable. We shall see in more detail in Part Two that this can take a nasty form at certain crisis points – reproduction, health care, partnership, divorce, child care and custody, for example. It also arises in the ordinary consumer market. Schwartz described the routine act of going into a shop to buy a new pair of jeans, knowing what jeans he had last time and therefore wanted again, only to be confronted with a large range of style options which left him flummoxed. Well, it may be said, wider fashions have caught up with the jeans market, and everything is now 'designer'. Buying clothes is about making choices *par excellence*.

The problem is that other consumer items are much more problematic. Choosing consumer durables – audio systems, televisions, washing machines, furniture and cars – is now an undertaking of such complexity that doing it seriously requires many hours of research. As noted earlier, one of the consumer society's leading features was the spread of ownership of consumer durables, which led, in 1957, to the foundation of the Consumers' Association which, through its magazine *Which?*, has attempted to provide comparative information, not only about the different products on offer, but about how durable they are. Since 1974 the Office of Fair Trading (OFT) has existed to protect consumers from abuses: to regulate the provision of credit, to ensure that sales and discounts are not bogus, and to promote codes of conduct and obtain legislation that have gradually extended consumers' rights. In broad terms it is now the case that for significant purchases, and in practice for many less significant, there is a right to return the product and obtain a refund for a limited period, in order to combat high pressure sales techniques, and to protect the naïve customer who acts on impulse. For some years the OFT also supported the agreement of codes of conduct by industry associations representing the sector, which attempted to ensure that the customer was treated fairly, and to outlaw specific oppressive and exploitative tactics characteristic of the sector. The culprits targeted were those which had given notorious trouble, such as second-hand car dealers and double glazing salesmen, as well as less troublesome ones. Recently the OFT has moved away from codes of practice, in the recognition that their objective is primarily the defence of the sector and its traders and that, whilst the promotion of good practice is beneficial, codes of practice lack the sanctions powerful enough to enforce it, and that redress procedures for aggrieved customers are mainly directed at conciliation rather than compensation, and may involve inordinate delay. More widely the raft of consumer legislation since 1945 provides a substantial and universal safety net, with the Small Claims Court, established in 1966, available to customers who want their money back and cannot get it otherwise.

The significance of consumer protection, for which there has been a government minister since the 1960s, is that it recognises the potential of consumer choice to overwhelm the customer and for the diversity of products and their features to be used to bamboozle the public. Market choice works by getting customers to discriminate good, or better, products and services from bad, or worse, so that, in time, the good drives out the bad. There are, however, many circumstances in which this cannot work. In the case of food, for example, adulterated or contaminated food may be sufficiently dangerous to ensure that those who buy it never return to the marketplace or are seriously damaged. For this reason the sale of food has been regulated for centuries. Modern consumer protection has arisen in part from a similar concern with safety – microwaves that do not leak radiation for example, and television sets that do not explode, as early models regularly used to do. Hazardous children's toys, usually imported from the Far East, are still a regular Christmas news item.

Modern consumer protection has, however, mainly derived from two other sources. First, a larger financial commitment means that the significance of any abuse is greater. With the spread of affluence, more of the population has the capacity to make major purchases. Secondly, the complexity, especially of modern consumer durables, is such that the lay public cannot be expected to understand how they work and to discriminate good from poor materials and construction, and quality or reliability of performance. Whereas the basis of the marketplace transaction is that the onus is upon the buyer to appraise the product carefully before buying it, and thereafter to accept the consequences of his having done so (*caveat emptor*, let the buyer beware), consumer protection significantly rebalances this arrangement because the buyer no longer has the knowledge, in many cases, to take the necessary precautions.

Nonetheless, the object of sellers is to obtain sales and the game in the marketplace continues, with sellers offering ever 'improved' products and services, and buyers considering whether they are tempted by the idea and the price. Discounts, sales, special offers, special credit terms, extended warranties, extended return and refund periods, and other tactics, as well as the blandishments of advertising and of sales staff, are used to entice customers and to find ways round consumer protection (sale items are not returnable for example). The outcome is the familiar, sustained culture of consumption frenzy; the constant expectation of the next purchase and the constant tweaking of cupidity for the next product, especially when others already have it. Such is the normality and comprehensiveness of this culture that most people are unaware of it. We pay attention to it, we think, when it suits us, and at times enjoy going out into the markets and looking for a good offer. The world in which such consumerism was unheard of is long gone. That was a world in which a new pair of boots or shoes was a major consideration, a purchase to be saved for and the money finally to be taken to the shoemaker to have a new pair made, which would be expected, with repairs, to last a good many years. Such antiquated ideas now persist only in the highest reaches of society where, for example, it is considered rather degrading to have to buy furniture: one would expect to have furniture in the family and to take care of it. At the other end of society the abandoned sofa has become a notorious item in derelict front gardens and fly tipping sites.

The importance of consumer protection, therefore, is that it is now a quite powerful institution that exists in recognition of the inability of consumers to make the necessary discriminations to allow markets to function effectively. The partial reversal of *caveat emptor* has underpinned consumer confidence and substituted for the inevitably limited extent of their knowledge. The limits of individual citizens' knowledge, and of their capacity to process information, also have implications in other directions, notably in the case of specialist services. Consumer protection derived not only from the need for remedy by consumers without protection and from their lack of capacity for informed choice. It also derived from systematic, widespread and persistent abuse of consumers by sellers: the Trade Descriptions Act 1968 for example was a landmark piece of legislation requiring goods and services to be as they are described and presented.

Professionals and other experts: intermediaries[1]

Increasingly we rely on those with complex specialist knowledge and skills to provide services to maintain our way of life: to fix the central heating boiler, repair the television, manage the sale of our homes, educate our children, attend to our health. The market could prevail here and in many areas demonstrated competence and value for money does secure reputation, and hence more customers. Many people have their cars maintained and their hair cut on this basis. Many more buy services in complementary and alternative medicine, where the personal risks may range from ineffectiveness – the calming and revitalising effect of the essential oils may be only transitory – to dangerousness, as with some herbal remedies and the incautious use of dietary supplements. The solution to these problems has historically been accreditation, the organisation of service providers into associations which provide training up to an agreed standard of competence, which then enables the trade body to accredit practitioners as competent. Of course, some are still more skilled than others, and many will specialise in specific topics within the trade, and on this basis reputations can be built and more informed consumer choices made. The process of what in its fullest version is *professionalisation* has continued relentlessly, but the consumer society has subjected it to something of a crisis.

On the one hand, the diversification and growth of knowledge has continued at an ever faster pace and the complexity of the products and services, not only on offer, but taken for granted by large numbers in the population, has increased vastly. Coupled with the natural tendencies of workers to seek intrinsic satisfaction from the work they do, and therefore the mastery of the knowledge and skills necessary for a job well done, as well as the equally natural desire for a fair recompense for the skill, time and effort expended on the service, this has led to an increasingly widespread use of accreditation. This has been reinforced by the growth of consumer protection, which has come to insist in more and more areas on minimum standards of competence, whether by formal state supervision and supervised licensing, as with gas and electrical installation for example, or by training schemes and accreditation organised by the industry. On the other hand, the specialisation of everyone has been met with consumer scepticism about the 'cosiness' of the barriers to open market competition thereby erected. The fully established professions – lawyers, doctors, accountants, surveyors, pharmacists and others – have achieved control over the recruitment, training and accreditation of the members of the occupation, along with the power to discipline and expel them for incompetence and misconduct. Those professions have also achieved state recognition that only their accredited members are entitled to perform certain services. Public antagonism to them has grown substantially in the past two generations. While in the 1950s professions were seen as repositories of benign, specialised knowledge underpinning vital services dispensed with skill and dedication and an unequivocal commitment to standards of service to the lay client, they are now seen as ruthless money-making businesses of decidedly variable competence and concern for clients.[2] The public who are constrained to call on them in situations of real need would be much happier if they believed the outcomes were more certain. For one of the downsides of sophisticated knowledge for the layperson is the capacity of the professional to manipulate it after the event to explain failure to deliver the desired outcome: the operation was successful, but the patient died; your case was a strong one, but the judge or jury took against you.

The notion that professions are cosy monopolies that need to be exposed to market forces to increase client choice and drive down prices has hence coincided with the contrary requirement for more services to be regulated and accredited, to ensure consumer protection. Whilst the latter has had the effect of driving up standards of service provision, and of course increasing its costs, the former has forced professional practice sharply in the direction of 'ordinary business'. Its concern is increasingly with costs, efficiency, throughput, value for money, cashflow and client income. Decisions on service are accordingly driven less and less by what the client needs, and more by what the practice can afford to provide. In the meantime clients have become more market conscious and more willing to explicitly shop around for professional services to drive down prices. Clients are more educated and more able to locate relevant knowledge and confront professionals with it: doctors now regularly wince at the sight of yet another patient clutching a sheaf of computer printout from the internet.

The enormous growth of knowledge has enabled the emergence of the consumer society and the manic spread of choice, but it has grown well beyond the capacity of the public, even a more educated and informed one, to keep pace with it. Choice increasingly has to be mediated by experts in order for it to be exercised rationally, whether this be through the services of professionals both knowledgeable and skilled at applying knowledge to individual circumstances, or through knowledge collators, who perform the market information searches that ordinary consumers do not have the time, skills or specialist knowledge to do. In a good many cases they do not know what information to seek out. Whether this intermediation takes the professional form, where the intermediary takes on your problem and seeks to resolve it; whether a lesser advice service is offered, for example by an insurance broker; whether the advice is simply made available, as it is in the fast growing range of market comparison websites; or whether those seeking advice resort to the ever proliferating range of self-help books, some offering practical help, others more nebulous nostrums,[3] the place of intermediaries in choice is widespread and important. Intermediaries do not provide the alternatives to choice that provision does: the decision in the end still rests with the customer or client. They do offer (and of course not all deliver on the offer in terms of competence or integrity) to take some of the effort and the uncertainty out of choices, particularly significant ones. In so doing they draw our attention once again to the fact that choice in all areas, baldly offered to the average citizen, may be less of an advantage and more a trap for the unwary or the untutored. Whilst the consumer economy and culture is enjoining all to get out and make more choices, and thus drive the economy and society forward – all these improved services are, after all, better, part

—

of progress – the consumer is, in an increasing range of circumstances, left exhaustedly asking: 'How do I do it successfully? Please do it for me, or give me some advice.'

Meanwhile competitive market pressure on those who provide specialist services is pushing them further and further in the direction of seeing clients as customers, and clients' problems as revenue earning opportunities. Consideration of whether a person's problem can really be dealt with effectively by their practice, or even whether the problem can be addressed by the professional at all, take second place to the need for revenue and throughput. All of this is not to say that greater choice and an emphasis on market forces has not sharpened up some of the professions and eliminated restrictive practices which had resulted in feather-bedding, notably gentlemanly restrictions on competition, advertising and scale fees. But the simple extension of choice in the consumer marketplace falls foul of the vast growth of knowledge, in its extent, complexity and specialised character.

An extreme example of this is provided in education, where, for example, university students are now widely expected to choose the courses they take as part of their degree, rather than be given a programme of courses necessary to acquiring knowledge and competence in the discipline. Similar processes have taken place at secondary level, designed to present material in an enticing and engaging way, and to make it more easily intellectually accessible. Drawing more students into engaging with a given subject is clearly desirable, but doing so through packaging, marketing and simplifying courses like so many products has contributed to widespread 'dumbing down' of secondary and university education. It fails to grasp the fact that students cannot yet know what they need to learn in order to gain understanding of a discipline. Only those who have mastered it know that and are capable of taking students through what is necessary to achieve it. 'Pick and mix' choices of attractive topics will achieve little learning. Yet why has this dramatic shift taken place ever more rapidly over the past forty years? In brief because the education market has swung from being a highly selective sellers' one, where only a designated few were allowed in to the upper end of secondary education at A levels and on to higher education, and hence could be put through the necessary intellectual hoops on pain of being rejected if they failed to get through them. It is now a vastly oversupplied buyers' market, in which institutions are desperate to recruit every last candidate, regardless of ability and motivation, with the added fear of financial penalties for failing them. Dumbing down in this market environment is not just inevitable, it is a leading requirement. Students exercise entirely spurious choices in the process, a fact to which the increasing levels of dropouts is testimony: the experience of uninformed choice leading to an uninforming education is confusing and dispiriting. It is notable that the subjects with the strictest disciplinary burden of intellectual hierarchy – linear subjects such as maths and science, where understanding at one level is an essential precondition of understanding at another – are suffering disproportionately in the market for student numbers, in relation to 'network' subjects such as the arts, humanities and social sciences, where learning progresses by making connections between different topics (but relies on working through a considerable number in order to achieve real understanding). Most successful are the non-disciplinary topic-based courses where 'pick and mix' offers few disadvantages, such as business studies and leisure and tourism. In sum, once again, if the citizen wishes to spend time, in this case two years at A level and three years at university, collecting information this is relatively unproblematic. If he wants to learn to understand a discipline, however, he needs to be subjected to a programme of learning in which room for choice is limited.

Provision

Somewhat different problems are posed by the creation of choices in situations where unified provision is more appropriate. Situations and judgements on them vary, but the extension of choice into areas where it is counterproductive has, in recent years, become more frequent and looks set to become more so. The problem with provision in the consumer market society we inhabit and sustain is that the practical issues surrounding individual cases become confused with concerns about monopoly and about state control, and hence take us back into debates about whether a state-managed economy is better than one delivered through private enterprise, and then into those about capital and class. Whether a service is best delivered by a single provider or left for market competition to sort the good from the bad is, in some circumstances, a separate issue from whether the provider is the state or the private sector (in any case subject to extensive state regulation today). Further examples illustrate the benefits of provision and the limitations of competition.

Queuing

A simple example of the benefits of provision as opposed to competition is provided by queuing. At some airport check-ins you have to choose which queue to join. Only too often your choice of the desk with the shortest queue is shown to be mistaken as a passenger in front of you engages in endless debate about seating, excess baggage or booking terms, necessitating lengthy inquiries by the check-in clerk. Sometimes, however, all passengers are put into a single queue, which is then serviced by all the available desks, so that everyone benefits from the average rate of progress. Post offices have also introduced this technique, although supermarkets have not, largely for reasons of space. The advantage is clear: no one knows who the problematic clients will be and therefore which queue will be the slowest; unifying everyone resolves the problem.

Directory enquiries and missing persons

Privatisation of telephone services in the 1980s produced increasing and gradually effective competition in Britain, which raised standards of service and reduced prices (although it should be added that privatisation took place at a critical point in the transformation of telephony by the introduction of digital exchanges and other equipment, and just before the introduction of mass-market mobile phones). This created a huge market opportunity for businesses willing to invest, and British Telecom was freed by privatisation to borrow extensively to do so. In the longer term one of the few remaining services on which BT retained a monopoly was directory enquiries. This remained an effective, rapid and reliable service, although it moved from being free under the old state monopoly to being charged for and, unsurprisingly, prices rose. The service was therefore opened to competition on the basis that this was simple: operators could use a computerised database to locate numbers, and efficiency would be rewarded by increased custom and lower prices. In practice the service disintegrated. From being a service with a single established number – 192 – it diversified into an increasing array of providers. Few phone users can remember the numbers and have even less idea of the costs, which vary in detail from provider to provider. Competition has destroyed service, with operators being required to process customers at unrealistic rates. A useful service has effectively been lost. It could have been secured by leaving it in BT's hands and controlling charges by regulatory oversight. Instead the ideology of choice prevailed.

A contrasting example is provided by the response to the problem of people who disappear. This has been a distressing problem for generations, and the numbers of missing persons have increased in recent decades. The police have, of course, an interest if there are suspicions of foul play, but they point out that, in the first place, people often take off for a while to escape their problems and, in the second, distressing as it is to family and friends, individuals have the right to disappear, and some people do. Further difficulties are posed by the autonomy of the police forces, all of which have their own missing persons lists, and their own procedures and priorities for investigating the necessary cases. Here was a clear case for provision where none existed.

The National Missing Persons Helpline was set up in 1992 to fill the gap.[4] As a charity it had difficulty in maintaining secure funding and in recent years has been helped with some government cash in recognition of the importance of its work. It now handles 150,000 calls a year and helps to resolve 70% of the cases it works on. By accumulating experience and expertise over time it has been able to develop skills in tracing missing people, and to offer advice and comfort to those abandoned. It offers the option of contact with families and friends to those traced, but without compulsion. It also collaborates with the police and other agencies in cases where people may be being held against their will, or may be vulnerable by virtue, for example, of emotional distress or mental confusion, domination

—

77

by powerful personalities or involvement in crime. Here we have an example of provision arising because of demand, but with the advantage of being able to be broad-based and focused on providing a service in respect of this single problem. As with all charities, the disadvantage is that it can do less than it would like, and has no state authorised powers. As ever, the rich can supplement provision, in this case by hiring private detectives as the marketplace-based alternative.

Railways

Similar arguments can be made on a much larger scale in respect of other services widely used by the public. Whatever one's views on the privatisation of British Rail (which was, incidentally, nationalised in 1948 because the then existing private railway companies had found it hard to remain profitable, as well as because the rail system was an inevitable target under clause four of the Labour Party's constitution), the break-up of the system into dozens of companies is now seen as disastrous by almost all except government spokesmen. Opinion polls and the Labour Party conference have repeatedly favoured re-nationalisation. State or private ownership is less the issue than the competition between the companies operating in the same national railway system. All have interests in avoiding costs and increasing revenues, and hence all have attempted to pass costs on to others and to garner as much income as possible, whether from passenger fares or state subsidies. The resulting madness sees lines axed because companies avoid taking on passengers to concentrate on more profitable routes, station platforms too short to accommodate the carriages necessary to accommodate all passengers, and station providers with no incentives to increase their length. The extra carriages themselves are a wheeze to collect additional fares at low costs by putting on fewer, longer trains instead of increased services. Ticketing has become increasingly incomprehensible as different companies compete to promote their routes, with special offers only available in limited time windows. Trains have become grossly overcrowded as companies seek to run trains that have largely pre-booked (and hence prepaid) seats like an aircraft, and are then forced to cope with the last-minute demand for travel, and extra trains and rolling stock cannot be provided on a system with limited track, as extra buses can on a road.

Anyone who has seen the railway system struggle over the past decade is hard put to deny its irrationalities. The case for single integrated provision, either by the state or the private sector, is overwhelming and is accepted in other countries. The argument for integrated provision does not need to reference the problems of the ill-fated Rail Track; problems which derived from the move from the state to the private sector and the characteristic abuses that then took place. British Rail, as a state industry, maintained its track to provide a safe and increasingly speedy service. Rail Track inherited the complete national rail network but, as a private business, charged the passenger carrying companies for the use of the track. It abused its position grossly by sacking staff to cut costs, contracting out maintenance services and then having no effective control over whether the maintenance was being done properly (as opposed to just cheaply). It failed to invest adequately in improving and adding to the system to encourage increased use of the track. The outcome has been a series of major rail crashes, massive public subsidies, years of speed restrictions and huge delays in track improvements. It is not the result – even avid privatisers did not quite go that far – of breaking the national track network up into separate lines owned by different companies. The mistake lay rather in failing to recognise that a railway system is just that, an integrated network of track and train services that need to be provided together.

Schools

Similar, but much simpler, arguments can be made in respect of education. At nursery level schools are small, and hence several may be within easy reach of a family. The state has, in recent years, encouraged private sector provision for the pre-school years and increasingly offered subsidies and tax breaks to providers and parents. It is now expanding state provision, with the aim of providing for all children from the age of three upwards – a laudable goal. As a result of this there is some over-provision in those areas where the private sector

—

has flourished and there are complaints of a crisis. One might argue here that, subject to the overall constraints of standards, competition might be permitted, if not encouraged. It is not, however, altogether obvious why nursery teachers should be motivated to do their job better because they may lose their jobs if their nursery school becomes unpopular. One rather suspects that nursery teachers do their job because they like it and will do it better if they are adequately funded and can predict next year's intake, thereby enabling more effective provision. As with many jobs, service and the intrinsic rewards of the work exist alongside profit and pay as a motive for working better. Nonetheless, children who are in a nursery school that is on a downward trend for whatever reason can be transferred to a better one, although with some disruption, and care must be taken to ensure that shifts in parental sentiment do not result in a stampede in which one school is emptied whilst another is overwhelmed. The key issue is catchment. The school run jams up roads badly enough already without more distant travel being required. If there are two nursery schools within walking distance there is room for choice.

With secondary schools this is not the case. Children with exceptional needs or abilities apart, families will want their children to go to the local school. Because secondary schools now need to be so large, in order to provide the range of facilities required, catchment areas are larger and distances travelled by pupils may be several miles. Yet the government now aspires to provide choice at secondary level, and derides the 'bog standard' comprehensive. It points out that the middle classes have always exercised choice by using their affluence. It does not consider carefully how they have done so: by moving into the catchment area of the school of their choice, that is, by still sending their children to the local school. There is no point in having a choice if distance prevents you from exercising it. What families need is a decent local school, not the necessity to travel a dozen miles to find one.

Even if the argument of competitive choice is accepted, where does this leave its victims? If the school begins to go downhill, alert parents with children who have just entered it may transfer them, despite the cost (not in money but in disrupted children). Those in the middle years, however, will be trapped by any exodus in a collapsing institution. The more and the faster this occurs, the more parents will panic and clamour to transfer their children, and the more the next nearest school will struggle to admit more pupils and to maintain standards: staff, buildings and playing fields cannot be purchased in short order like the latest fashions.

Yet the remedy is already present and could be used to try to stabilise the situation. Schools are already inspected, categorised, publicised and, *in extremis*, taken over and restarted. Will state schools just be abandoned because parents do not like the way they are run? It seems unlikely in practice that the state, and in particular those responsible for education at local level, will be content to abandon the children of less resourceful parents to schools in decline. Educational policy for the past twenty years has been driven by the very reverse objectives: to get standards everywhere up to an acceptable level, in other words, adequate provision for all.

Health care

Similar arguments in respect of the benefits of provision over disaggregation and competition can be made in respect of health care. As the biggest employer in Europe the NHS suffers from the disadvantages of size as well as reaping the benefits, for example, in bulk purchase of pharmaceuticals. The NHS has always been broken down into units delivering services at regional and local level, however. As with schools, the provision of specialist and hospital services has become increasingly complex and demanding, requiring concentration to deliver good results. The pattern has changed over time, but the principle has, until recently, remained the same: primary care is provided by GPs, with patients able to exercise some choice in their locality. More serious problems are treated by specialised care, delivered through hospital complexes, out-patient and in-patient, which serve cities and regions. Concerns about the ever increasing costs of medicine to the NHS, largely because of increased longevity of the population, coupled with rapid strides in intervention capacity involving increasingly sophisticated, and therefore expensive, equipment and drugs, were addressed by the new Right in the 1980s and 1990s with an attempt to use market principles to drive down costs. Artificial internal markets were created, which attempted to cost the use of resources and delivery of services. The accounting strategy behind this has proved effective in business in identifying where profits are being made and what activities are sustaining losses, but the remedy in business was not available to the NHS. If cardio-thoracic surgery is profitable, but psychiatry is not, you cannot decide to do more of the former but no more of the latter or, at least, you can, but that would violate the principle of the NHS to provide comprehensive health care. The outcome of the internal market foray was frustration for medical staff, huge amounts of time spent on additional form filling and the hiring of a new army of health service managers to enforce the system. It was unpopular and ineffective and was rejected by the incoming Labour government.

Its alternative has been to raise funding, recognising that the NHS provides one of the most efficient health care systems in the world, but that national spending per capita in Britain has been well below comparable economies. If it had more money, the NHS could be better staffed and equipped, and do its job properly and still efficiently. This, however, has not been seen as enough; the government believes that patients must now also have choice and this will benefit patients by enabling them to pursue the best treatment (although how they are to locate it is less than clear, other than through the proposed league tables of success which, if the school league tables are a guide, will be far from adequate).[5] The choice will also benefit the system by driving up standards, because patient choices will carry with them treatment and treatment will be funded, so patient choices will confer resources.

There are obvious difficulties with these proposals. Hospitals, clinics and doctors that are perceived as stars will attract adulation. Where matters may be literally those of life and death, people will queue up to get the best treatment. Those far enough up the queue may well receive better treatment than they would otherwise have done, but those further down will be subject to delays, which may be more damaging than getting immediately available treatment. Further, as the Audit Commission has noted,[6] patients deserting poor facilities reduce the income flows of those facilities and precipitate them further into deficit. These deficits can, under the new 'money follows the patient' rule, only be made good by closing down wards and sacking staff. As with schools, the end point of this process is either complete hospital closure, or remedy by inspection, reorganisation and external supervision. The difficulty with the NHS is that the relationship between the state and the medical profession is not the same as between the state and teachers. Teachers are state licensed and state employees. Doctors are much more independently managed by their professional bodies and contract with the NHS to provide services. Redirection and reorganisation of health is therefore much less easy for the state, which can only act in clinical matters via the medical profession.

To make matters worse, the government has opted to provide some services, such as MRI scans and some eye surgery, from private sector suppliers, which thus act as a marker for costs, forcing the NHS to takes costs more seriously, as well as giving extra capacity.[7] Once again the difficulty is the lack of oversight and control over private sector provision. There have been complaints that private providers have failed to interpret data from MRI scans properly so that NHS clinics have to repeat the analysis, that standards in eye surgery are variable, and that the private sector will only take on work which can be routinised and tightly costed (and made profitable), leaving complicated (and hence expensive) cases to be picked up by the NHS. As with the railways, the incentive upon one supplier in a multi-supplier system is to avoid costs and target revenue. Once again unified provision rather than an extension of choice has considerable advantages.

Issues of service as opposed to market values also impinge here. The costs of health care are now so great and increasing so fast that a rationing system has had to be introduced, presided over by the National Institute for Health and Clinical Excellence (NICE), which determines which new drugs and techniques should be nationally funded as demonstrably beneficial and value for money. At the front line of patient care, however, medical staff, on the whole, know what they want and why. They may want resources that they know are in short supply because of costs, but that is quite different from having to make complex decisions about costs and resources at every clinical decision point with a view to minimising the hospital trust's expenditure and maximising its revenue. Medical staff harassed by costs and administrative considerations are in a less favourable position to provide effective patient care. The costs of administering patient choice, both in staff morale and in money, could well be significant, quite apart from the chaotic imbalances that patient choice promises to unleash. As with schools, greater oversight, evaluation of resources, careful consideration of facilities and staff training, and careful effort to ensure appropriate levels of staffing would arguably pay greater dividends for the NHS as a whole. As in other markets, allowing choice to prevail for patients will ensure that the best informed, best advised and supported will get the best treatment, at the expense of those who have no advice, little support, little energy and limited capacity to process information, people, for example, who are seriously infirm or ill.

Pensions

A final example of choice being substituted for provision is pensions. Here lessons appear to be being learnt after twenty years of chaos. As was described earlier, the new Right was keen to address the pensions issue in the 1980s, because of the rising costs of the state pension and the likely failure of occupational pensions to benefit many workers because of increased rates of job change (the end of 'jobs for life'). In 1986 the government therefore legislated to promote personal pensions, with tax breaks and a National Insurance rebate as incentives for people to take them up. Most private pensions were provided by insurance companies and banks. Pension providers responded to the new market opportunity with gusto, and engaged in systematic abuse of customers.[8] As will be indicated below, some of this was all but inevitable, given the circumstances.

The need in respect of pensions, then as now, is to ensure that the entire population has a degree of financial security when they stop working. The new Right was enthused with the notion of individual self-reliance and the virtues of markets, and hence was keen to promote it in respect of pensions. It argued that the state pension could not be properly funded and that, in any case, the system that had emerged through occupational schemes was one where everyone expected a second pension, in which they took a more active part, to supplement state provision. In the more dynamic markets this could not work for everyone, hence the need for personal pensions. This ignored the earlier remedy to the problem, the State Earnings Related Pension Scheme (SERPS), which offered to address the issue of job change by allowing employers to pay into a state scheme rather than an occupational one. The provisions of many occupational schemes, at least for many of their employees, were better than SERPS, but for those without an occupational scheme it was a remedy. The government pointed out that the pay-out under SERPS might not be as good as personal private schemes, a point not difficult to illustrate in a period of relatively high inflation, with good stock market returns. People should therefore have the right to go down the personal private pension route.

This did not take account of likely outcomes. Private providers compete with one another and, in doing so, some will do better than others. That means that some will also do worse. How is the young worker to decide? The only obvious guide to this was the size and track record of the provider but, as the regulatory body in charge of the sector was eventually driven to require advertisers to state, past record is not a certain guide to the future. In the case of pensions this is no trivial matter. On the one hand pensions provide security at a point when citizens can no longer work to provide it; on the other it is very far into the future, perhaps thirty or forty years, further than any other financial issue about which citizens are expected to make decisions. How, then, is anyone to make a reasonably informed estimation of which pension provider to go with? The state by contrast can give undertakings, and is usually to be relied upon to deliver on them. Things are much less certain than this, however. Over a longish period of time private enterprises, even the most august and established financial institutions, change. They venture into new areas, like estate agency, as many did in the 1980s and 1990s, in which they collectively lost billions. They may be taken over by other firms; their management, once staid and reliable, is replaced by those more adventurous and less meticulous. They fall foul of rogue employees, just as Barings Bank did to Nick Leeson. No matter how good a personal pension provider may look today, no one has the slightest idea how they will perform in thirty years' time. Private pension provision is hence a blind bet, which may be all very exciting when it is £50 on the Grand National, but not quite the same amount of fun when it is your pension.

So it has proved, even over the brief span of the last decade or two. Stock markets have fallen and inflation rates have been tamed and, in consequence, pension plan yields are now far below their projections from the 1980s and 1990s. What do you do? The opportunity cost is huge. If you had saved more earlier you would be secure; to save enough now may be impossible. Many of the providers have indeed become far less successful and attractive than they were: competition and market changes have given them a real battering. One example, however, stands out.

Equitable Life was an insurer with a track record going back two hundred years. Such were its skills in the post-war period that it rose to pre-eminence as the 'posh' person's life assurance and pensions provider. Top people saved with Equitable Life and looked forward to a comfortable retirement. Unfortunately, it became dominated by a rather forceful chief executive who was convinced of the merits of his own ideas and would brook no opposition. He decided that a further boost could be given to Equitable's market position by taking advantage of its financial strength and its proven capacity to deliver by offering what other companies dared not.

Insurance based pensions operate as saving schemes based on pooled investments. Hence the risks of investing in the stock market are spread very much more widely than ordinary investors could manage and yet the benefits of the higher long-term yields of equities can be obtained. The outcome is a lump sum cash pay-out that increases the more skilled the insurer is at its job. This is very nice for the pensioner, but most do not want to just spend the money for fear that it will run out, so a pension is obtained by selling the cash sum to an annuity provider, often an insurer or a bank, who in return provides an annual cash sum until death. This means that the annuity provider has to conjecture how long annuitants will survive and how much can be made by investing the cash in the meantime. The latter figure depends upon markets', primarily stock and bond markets', future performance. Problems are therefore posed for the prospective pensioner in respect of how buoyant markets are when his insurance scheme matures and he has the cash sum to convert into an annuity. If market yields are poor, the annuities on offer for the same sum will be much less than if they are buoyant. Equitable claimed that it was so successful that it could ignore this, and could offer guaranteed annuity rates when insureds signed up for their pension savings policies. This therefore had the significant advantage of certain provision: savers knew how much pension they would get for how much savings, at least if they were prepared to take a bet on how much Equitable would pay out for a given period and amount of monthly savings.

Guaranteed annuity rates proved to be a huge mistake. In the changed market conditions at the turn of the century, not only were pay-outs lower, but expectations as to the future yields of markets were much lower, because inflation was not expected to rise again to the high levels of the 1990s, let alone the 1970s. The only way guaranteed rates could therefore be paid was by poaching the funds that would have been used to pay other insureds. Equitable went to court to try to back out of guaranteed annuity rates and lost. The outcome was Equitable's collapse into financial chaos and ignominy, and the serious disadvantaging of thousands of pension savers.[9]

In the idea of guaranteed annuity rates Equitable implicitly recognised the importance of secure provision for pensions but, even as a large and successful private company, it could not ensure it. Government thinking now seems gradually to be moving back in the direction of state provision, the difficulty still being how big the universal state pension should be and whether everyone should be compelled to make contributions to a state scheme in order to provide either a supplementary or enhanced basic pension. The policy problem is filling the gap between a state pension which is increasingly inadequate and the beneficiaries of successful occupational schemes, who have reasonably comfortable pensions. How to provide for those who either do not have the continuity of employment, or who have low incomes for much of their lives, and either way cannot save enough to fund a significant supplementary pension is an unsolved problem. As with other problems of provision, security is the primary issue. If the private sector is involved, it will have to be underwritten by the state. So far the Labour administration has made several initiatives, but none have really worked.

Popular music and broadcasting: counter-examples?

Let me be clear that my argument is not that choice, or increased choice, is never desirable, desired or beneficial. Not only, as we have seen in Chapter Two, will individuals have their own appetites and comfort zones for making more or fewer choices, but the effectiveness of choice as an institution varies from case to case. The interest of these two cases lies in the source of the increased choice: the digitalisation of information, and the use of the internet to provide distribution and access.

The central argument of Anderson's account of the impact of the internet on pop music is that it has all but blown away the music industry's capacity to produce hits and to promote individuals and groups to star status.[10] Consumers now have access to a mind-boggling range of music, which they can acquire personally at no or low cost by downloading from specialist sites and by file sharing. This has made serious inroads into the music industry's profitability but, despite sustained efforts, it has been unable to control the shift in consumption. Consumer choice has been further fortified by participation in review and recommendation via internet blogs, which not only reduce search costs, but have turned the search into a personal exploration of what satisfies the individual and a rewarding process in itself. This is further secured by the possibility of sampling tracks and by the ability to select the best or favourite tracks, rather than being committed to an entire album. The outcome has been a shift from hits to niches, the fragmentation of the audience into thousands of specialised interests (a 'long tail' in Anderson's term), all of which can be sustained by the efficiency of the internet in distribution and access, and by the benefits of modern digital equipment in making the production and recording of music easier and cheaper.

Aficionados will want to argue the details of this process. I will accept Anderson's picture of choice being increased by the internet and that that development is much appreciated by the audience for popular music. Sometimes choice, and more choice, works. My reservations are about the implications that he claims. Much the same is happening in publishing and film he argues, and I suggest that similar arguments apply to the current debate on public service broadcasting. The question is whether pop music is a typical case of a general change, or a special case. I believe there are grounds for suggesting the latter.

In respect of pop music itself there are two grounds for caution about generalising: the nature of the audience and the history of pop music.[11] It plays an important part in the life of the young. Even though older people may maintain an interest, it is largely the young who create pop music, who are emotionally sustained by it and who can now spend significant proportions of their days listening to it thanks to the quality of modern personal music players. To put it simply, the young, as the prime audience, are motivated to search for the music that 'does it for them' and, it might be added, that in most cases they have the leisure time to engage in searching for new music that is less available to their older contemporaries. Not only do the young have the motivation to look for niche music, the history of pop music has pushed the iPod generation in just that direction.

When rock and roll emerged in the 1950s it was developed by a music industry that saw an expanding market. Young people had more money in their pockets as post-war affluence spread, and records and record players were produced more cheaply to tap into the youth market. For perhaps twenty years a kind of mainstream prevailed under the tutelage of an increasingly powerful music industry, but, by the latter 1970s, notably with the arrival of punk, which deliberately resisted the major recording companies as a base, pop music began a progressive process of fracture. Its musical sources in blues, rhythm and blues, country music and folk music had themselves never disappeared, and were rediscovered. Influences from outside the Anglo-American musical axis increasingly contributed, first reggae, then an explosion of world music. Internally local differentiation took place: ska, northern soul, garage, hip-hop and many others, some of these genres spreading further than others. The centre could not hold and by the 1980s mainstream pop music was in decline. It survived because the music industry sustained it, but the decline was progressive. Now the young look not only for something new and special, but range over the entire history of pop music and related genres over half a century and more. The internet has made this much easier and cheaper, and given new life to record companies' backlists.

Anderson may be right about what has happened to pop music then, but not necessarily about the implications of it. The internet has been more a catalyst than the driver of change. To be sure, as a result of the developments that it assisted, the capacity of the music industry to continue to play the role of central provider has greatly weakened, but choice always was the main driving force in pop music, despite the industry's efforts at the provision. Much the same can be said of Anderson's claim that the same will happen in publishing. He points out that of nearly two hundred thousand books a year published in English ninety per cent will not make it into mainstream bookshops, and that the average book in America sells around five hundred copies. The vast majority of books published will not make money for the publishers or authors: touché. As he acknowledges, publication can have other benefits, such as promoting the reputation of the author, but, fundamentally, authors write because they have something they want to put into the public domain: to entertain, to instruct, to inform, or to stimulate debate. As the costs of publication are driven down by new technology and an ever more diversified market sustained by the internet, the argument goes, publishing is developing its own long tail. This presupposes that progressively more people will buy more books about increasingly recondite subjects, yet publishers are constantly bemoaning the costs and difficulties of producing and marketing material. True, the larger publishers are arguably too focused on the blockbuster hits on which they spend too much in advances to authors and on publicity, and, to that extent, are as obsessed with hits as the music industry. Anderson's argument, however, presumes that there is a much larger and very diverse book buying market for even the most specialised work. Any publisher will respond that this may conceivably be the case, but that first you have to reach such markets efficiently which, it is claimed (but not yet demonstrated), can be done by the internet, and secondly you have to supply the books.

—

90

This can be a bit of a problem. Most people can read, and most can write for practical purposes, but only limited numbers are able and willing to write at length, and only a minority of them can do so competently. More could no doubt achieve competence, but that would require time, effort, training and above all critical engagement with those with the knowledge, skills and understanding of the topics in question. Almost everyone has views and can express them, but even a casual review of the contributions to internet notice boards and blogs suggests limited literacy, knowledge, insight and acumen. Who is going to write long tail books in a way that will stimulate readers to buy them and encourage their friends to buy them?

Somewhat similar arguments, although buttressed by others that have been mentioned in connection with earlier topics, apply to broadcasting. It too is being subjected to the pressures of digitalisation, which has permitted a sudden proliferation of channels and the capacity to override programming schedules and summon up programmes on demand. The logic is similar to the long tail argument: digitalisation has vastly increased the power of consumer choice. A different question is posed in respect of broadcasting, however: will the endless proliferation of specialist channels destroy public service broadcasting? It seems that this is very likely, and the more important question is therefore: what will be the cost? To answer this question the BBC invited Stephen Fry and Sir David Attenborough to give their views.[12]

The response of these sophisticated and long-serving public service broadcasters is interesting as much for what it does not quite include as for what it does. There is a straightforward argument for provision, based on the claim that a significant proportion of the public does not want to devote itself exclusively to specialised topics, but rather wants to be entertained, informed and engaged by a channel which offers both quality and diversity of programmes. They do not want to choose; they want to switch on and see what happens. Nevertheless, some programmes will be much more successful than others, not just because the genre has wider appeal, but also because of inevitable variation in programme quality. The BBC faced a challenge essentially similar to the current one when ITV began to compete with it in the 1950s. Even though the popular game shows and soaps that ITV used to achieve high ratings were seen as beneath the BBC's dignity, ratings competition was unavoidable. The solution was to continue to use licence fee money to make programmes that were seen as worthy contributions to national life and culture, even if not necessarily popular, but to sustain ratings by also making popular programmes. The trick was to avoid viewers switching channels by 'hammocking' a less popular programme between two popular ones and, latterly, with the advent of more BBC channels, screening a more specialist programme initially on BBC2 (or 3 or 4) and then repeating it, or running later episodes or series, on BBC1.

The point of interest about the strategy which is not acknowledged explicitly by either Fry or Attenborough is that it is educational, and in that respect elitist: Auntie knows best. Programme makers and network managers are commissioning programmes that they believe are not only going to be of good quality, but in the public interest – beneficial to society. Public service broadcasting endeavours to entice a (partially reluctant) public to take an interest in things it would not immediately have thought of itself. In this they have been remarkably successful, and not, of course, just by bamboozling their naïve audiences with paternalistic propaganda. A significant part of their audience wants to be informed, stimulated and challenged by material which they have not come across before, and is pleased to be shown how and why it is important. They would not necessarily know how to go about finding out about it for themselves and would not necessarily, for example, have the necessary expertise in science, medicine, history or current affairs to know how or where to look (internet or no internet). Public service broadcasting, in other words, acts at its best like a huge cultural and political filter. Only a really large organisation with a wide range of expert staff can constantly trawl through everything going on in the world and make informed judgements about what is important to get across to the public.

To dismantle this system, then, is not to give the public what it wants. It is to deprive the public of what it would want, but does not yet know about. To claim that the market will show what has popular support is subterfuge. People cannot constitute themselves as an audience if they do not know what they are looking for. As far as much of the public is concerned many significant new developments

—

are what Donald Rumsfeld called 'unknown unknowns'.[13] Public service broadcasting is hence a vital form of provision. Its decline into multiple specialist channels would, first, be likely to limit funding for their output and thereby probably compromise programme quality in a good many cases and, secondly, deny a large section of the public access to material that it now appreciates through public service broadcasting. Of course it can be argued that sooner or later vital topics would surface and be addressed and debated in the mainstream of politics and culture. Debate about channel proliferation leading to a lowest common denominator model of broadcasting apart, the political risk is that in the absence of public service broadcasting, too much important material would surface too little and too late. Broadcasting could develop into a diversified long tail like pop music, but there are good reasons, and an established appreciative audience, for it to remain as a vital form of public provision.

Realistically, however, the proliferation of channels is not going to be reversed, nor is the availability of programmes to be watched at the viewer's time of choice, so undermining the art of the schedulers. Further, the rising generation consumes television output alongside the use of websites (increasingly with video footage), computer games and films, which are also likely to be available from the internet. There were fears that radio broadcasting, when it began, would marginalise print journalism, and similarly that television would supersede radio and print. Neither has happened, but there has been an impact and audiences' time is not unlimited. The different modes of access imply an inevitable increase in deliberate choice in watching television, and a challenge to simple provision and the passive viewer prepared to be entertained. The key issue is whether public service broadcasting can maintain its capacity for strength in depth and its concentration of talent. Relentless outsourcing and political challenges to the licence fee system put this in question, but it is at present not clear at just what point the baby of quality, diversity and public interest will be flushed away with the bath water of cost-cutting and radically increasing viewer choice.

—

FIVE

Some wider problems with choice

The last chapter was concerned with the alternatives to choice as a mechanism through intermediaries (a partial alternative) and provision. Problems with choice in a consumer society arise very widely, however. Choice does not always work very well even if there is no readily available alternative. Sometimes these problems seem to be simply those of 'bad behaviour' – of people taking advantage – but on closer inspection turn out to be more entrenched and intractable. This chapter will look briefly at a number of examples, beginning with one that demonstrates the manipulation of choice in markets.

Cartels and competition

The preservation of choice in markets is secured by making them open to newcomers, so that competition is endemic. This is the basic mechanism for the advancement of the capitalist market economy. From the producer's point of view markets may present opportunities especially if you have a new idea or product, but at the same time other people's initiatives, which sustain the competition, are a risk. One solution for those who do not relish competition is to collaborate instead with their rivals. Cartels usually involve either price fixing or market sharing. Thus, competitors may agree not to compete on price, and allow markets to favour them as they will, confident that the quality of their goods or services will be adequate to give them a reasonable market share. Alternatively markets may be allocated to cartel members, for example by one firm being allowed to prevail in one country or region, or by contracts being allocated in turn to participants, with the preferred one submitting the lowest bid. Another variant of the same problem arises when one firm dominates the market, usually taken to mean having a fifty per cent or more share in trade. Such a firm can often determine prices and allow other market participants to operate only if they do not compete on price. Tactics include threatening to withdraw supplies to those who trade with uncooperative competitors, preventing raw materials being accessed by competitors by buying up suppliers and, if necessary, engaging in price wars designed to drive the competition out of the market. New competitors with new ideas and market strategies can often be tolerated for a while to see how they fare, and then can be bought up by the giant market leader by being made an offer they cannot refuse: either accept our generous terms or we will price you out of the market and poach your key staff.[1]

This is all very nasty, and is made worse by the fact that it routinely involves large and long-established firms. It constitutes the stifling of choice at the heart of market capitalism and it must surely be opposed. US governments have always been opposed to cartels, and legislation to ban them and outlaw their practices has been in place since the beginning of the twentieth century. Europe has been less militant, not least because governments have found it desirable to protect and promote the major firms in many sectors in order to ensure their contribution to the national economy, and to ensure their capacity to compete internationally. This inclination was well established by the early twentieth century and was reinforced by the need for reconstruction after the war. State support for major firms was a leading feature of the successful economic reconstruction of war-torn France, Germany and Japan for example. Britain has had a more pragmatic history of regulating cartels and market dominance. The Restrictive Practices Court was established in 1956, not to punish cartel participants, but to encourage those entering into such arrangements to register them with the court, which would then decide whether or not they were in the public interest.

In recent years the stance of both Britain and Europe has moved sharply towards antagonism and away from tolerance of cartels. The European Union Office of Competition now has the most extensive powers of any EU agency and may initiate investigations into any firm in any member state, with the power to enter premises, seize information and interrogate personnel without prior permission from the member state's government. The agency can also prosecute offenders before the European Court and impose fines of up to ten per cent of the firm's turnover. The agency has been quite energetic in recent years, taking action against suppliers of vitamins, for example, and against Microsoft. Similarly, the British Monopolies Commission has recently been transformed into the Competition Commission, with powers to investigate abuses on its own initiative rather than in response to complaints by the public or injured market traders, and with similarly substantial powers of investigation and sanction to its EU counterpart. Why this sudden enthusiasm?[2]

To understand this we have to look at why business is tending to market administration rather than competition. Anti-cartel sentiment is correct in suggesting that, for some businesses, a managed market is more attractive than a competitive one. It is more stable and secure for participants. Profit margins need not be greatly raised by cartel arrangements, but they are more reliable. Firms may be lazy and greedy, but many cartel members are not just that. A leading feature of industrial capitalism is that, as time goes on, as innovations in production and distribution cumulate, and competition takes its toll, the capital costs of participating in a market rise inexorably. The technology involved becomes very expensive and economies of scale significant. Competitors are gradually knocked out by failure and by takeover and merger, and markets end up dominated by a handful of firms. Hence, choice and competition is restricted.

New entrants may be able to get into markets where established participants become complacent and fail to spot new opportunities. This is exactly what Microsoft did when IBM derided the significance of the market for personal computers and remained content with its dominance of the market for ever larger mainframes. Similarly the rise of no frills, low-cost airlines in America created chaos among the established players and contributed to the eventual collapse of Pan-Am. Recall, however, that although Virgin Atlantic was eventually successful in establishing itself in competition with other transatlantic air carriers, notably British Airways in Britain, BA's track record was that of ruthless market dominance. The privatised BOAC and BEA first of all gobbled up British Caledonian, the existing private sector competitor, and then responded to the attempt to establish a low-cost

—

97

transatlantic service by Freddie Laker's Sky Train with price cutting which drove Laker out of business. Branson's Virgin had greater financial muscle, but BA maintained a long campaign of 'dirty tricks', exploiting its dominance of ticketing services, spreading false rumours and engaging in such skulduggery that Virgin eventually sued BA and won. The blaze of publicity did Virgin no harm, but the more important point is that it did not seriously harm BA either, which remains bigger and more prosperous, and still dominant in the British and European markets.

Competition becomes particularly problematic in situations in which there are limited numbers of market participants and where technology has become stabilised and innovations no longer forthcoming. This means that all participants have the same costs of production and distribution, and that competition therefore simply erodes profit margins as prices are cut to secure market share. The alternative to 'ruinous competition' is hence cartels. This has notoriously been the case in the markets for road surfacing – tarmacadam (black top) and cement. The inputs are standardised ingredients: tar, cement, sand and aggregate; plants for processing have standardised technology. Distribution has to be rapid, before the product goes off, and is by specialised lorries to the construction sites. Transport costs are hence high and economies of scale by having a centralised distribution of limited benefit. The outcome has been a series of regional cartel arrangements, pilloried for years by the Office of Fair Trading. Such problems are not the inevitable outcomes of having fewer participants in the market: competition between supermarkets in Britain has been very vigorous for example, even though their numbers have dwindled.

Restrictions on competition are, however, increasingly likely as more markets mature and become dominated by one or a few firms; hence the new found zeal of competition commissions in Britain and the EU. What this reminds us is that the international capitalist economy has moved in a direction in which such domination and its restrictive market practices are likely to become the norm, not the exception. Choice in the marketplace may increasingly become a choice between the products and services of one or a few perhaps colluding providers. Is this increasingly objectionable? Insofar as competition is the main driver of innovation, price cuts and market progress, yes, but this is not quite the whole story.

In respect of capacity to achieve control of markets branding can be seen as a legitimate parallel to cartels, which instead takes advantage of customer preference for the tried and tested. And branding is intended to play to the habit forming tendencies of customers. Some of the most valuable brands in the world – Coca-Cola, Heinz baked beans and tomato ketchup for example – have successfully held off competition, including these days from supermarkets' own brand products. Successful businesses trade on their established market presence, their track record and their ability to persuade customers that it is not worth the price margin of their competitors to try something different. Of course it can be argued that the existence of real competition exercises discipline on price, but the huge success of branding – unlike his airline, Branson's Virgin Cola did not succeed – shows that purchasers often want to shortcut widespread search and have a preference for security. This of course chimes with the aspiration of the larger corporations who, the more they come to be among the survivors in a maturing sector, seek additional market share less and less, and aim to preserve what they have more and more. They have a great deal to lose and have less and less to gain from defeating the competition, but more incentive to manage it.

Nor are the results of abuse of market dominance all bad. Microsoft was convicted of abusing the dominance of its Windows operating system software and required to divulge details of its code in order to allow competitors to offer, for example, a rival web browser, or music player. In a sector as dynamic and innovative as computing it would be foolish to stifle competition, and yet the personal computer market is made far simpler for the average user by the fact that Windows, in its successive versions, is by far the commonest operating system.

The problems of intervention

The outcomes of interventions to stop cartels and restrictive practices are also not necessarily benign. One of those accepted by the Restrictive Practices Court for many years was the net book agreement that allowed booksellers a thirty per cent margin from publishers in view of the peculiarities of book selling. Unlike, say, a clothes shop, which expects to clear its stock regularly, and will completely restock several times a year for the new seasons, a bookseller survives by having stock on the shelves for extended periods, because it is the range of books which attracts an adequate range of buyers. The shop is hence performing part of the function of the publisher's warehouse and the maintenance of shelves of books is clearly costly. The risk has always been that newsagents and supermarkets will offer to buy large quantities of best-selling titles, but demand deep discounts from the publishers. These titles will then be sold cheap, not only undercutting the specialist bookseller on price, but depriving him of the top slice of his revenue from the best-selling titles' sales, which would subsidise the stocking of lesser selling titles. Market changes recently have eroded the net book agreement and driven many small independent booksellers out of the market. Internet sales at large discounts have taken some market share and, because they are based in vast warehouses in remote locations, can outprice the high street bookseller on all titles. High streets themselves have been transformed by the rise of chains of booksellers competing successfully both with newsagents and with specialist independents: Ottakar's, Dillon's and Waterstone's have established themselves, expanded, competed and consumed one another and, together with supermarkets, have now driven most of the independents out of the market. If you want a book that your supermarket or newsagent does not stock, you may order it over the internet … if you are sure you know what you want. If you want to browse, you have to live in a town which is large enough to be served by one of the big chains. Book titles multiply and book sales continue, but the market has been steadily altered, and it now looks likely gradually to conform to the maturation process that has affected other industries, and be dominated by a few players.

Pubs and beer

A rather different example is provided by beer. Many areas in the UK were historically dominated by one local brewer, which had often built and continued to own the pubs. They had achieved control in the nineteenth century, because of the transport costs of delivering beer over longer distances in good condition. By the end of the 1980s the system of tied pubs, which required the landlord to serve the beer produced by the owner brewer had clearly become outdated. In the first place many local breweries had in practice been closed and the businesses taken over by a dwindling oligarchy of ever larger brewers. These produced beer in centralised locations, sometimes to local specifications, which were then branded with the old brewer's name and distributed nationally by road. The outcome was that the surviving brewers owned thousands of pubs and there were clear local monopolies. In addition, the surviving smaller brewers were likely to succumb to competition before much longer, not least because they were unable to offer their products in pubs owned by the oligarchs. The solution was obvious: the old system of tied pubs was an anachronism. The big brewers were eventually required to restrict themselves to two thousand pubs each. The pubs now released would boost the networks of the successful smaller breweries and would hopefully also allow the formation of a raft of free, untied pubs: some in smaller chains, some in individual ownership. In addition, all tied pubs were required to offer at least one guest beer to further increase competition and customer choice.

The response of the big brewers was to recognise that the profitability of many of their smaller pubs had been marginal for years, as drinkers increasingly deserted the local for wine bars, clubs and the supermarket. They concentrated their resources in the larger pubs in good locations, which they refurbished and themed. They resolved the problem of guest beers by doing deals with big foreign brewers, and accelerating the shift from ale to lager, with its higher prices and longer shelf life. Foreign brewers were keen to get into the British market, and supported their efforts with extensive advertising and promotion, managing to achieve a significant shift from draft to bottled beer, and to put a cachet and higher price tag on foreign beers. The outcome was that the number of pubs fell, and the price of beer rose substantially as brewers engaged in a further round of international takeovers and mergers. A few of the small independents survived.

That was not the end of the story, however. The beer orders and the big sell-off of pubs that they required led to the formation of the pub companies (pubcos). These own large numbers of pubs all over the country, which they either manage themselves or (mainly) lease to tenants, usually on a 10- to 20-year assignable lease with full repairing requirements. Not all tenants are tied to the pubco, that is required to buy their beer through them, but the six largest pubcos, with some 21,800 pubs between them, all operate a tie. The effect of this is that the immediate purpose of the beer orders, which were repealed in 2002 and 2003, has been achieved. There was a change in ownership of pubs in many localities and, more importantly for the consumer, a range of beers from different brewers is now available in many pubs. The pubcos use their size to negotiate with the major brewers to achieve large discounts on the beer, which they then arrange to distribute to their lessees. So far, so good. As the Commons Select Committee on Business and Enterprise found in their second report on the pubcos in five years,[3] however, these arrangements operate neither to the benefit of the public, nor of the lessees.

Half the discount achieved by the pubcos on beer is retained by them, meaning that, in addition to their fixed rent, they have a second income stream from the beer, which increases with the success of the pub. Further, they often insist on a tied arrangement for pub gaming machines and sometimes also for wines, spirits and soft drinks. The pubcos argue that they provide all manner of advice, support, marketing and training, and point out that the lease allows people to own a pub business, which they can sell on by assigning the lease, at close to a tenth of the cost of buying a pub. Against this the Committee found that only twenty five per cent of lessees were attracted by the cheapness of market entry, and most were attracted by the specific qualities of the pub. In research undertaken by the Committee sixty seven per cent of lessees earned less than £15,000 a year; even when the pub had a turnover of more than £500,000, more than fifty per cent earned less than £15,000 a year. As was pointed out, the bigger the discount the pubcos could negotiate with the brewers and other suppliers the larger their income, and it was hence in their interest for the list price to rise so that they could get larger amounts. The effect of this has been that the price of beer in pubs has risen by 3.3–3.5 times the off trade (supermarkets and off licences) price between 1998 and 2008. Not surprisingly, seventy eight per cent of lessees in the Committee's survey were unhappy with the tie. The Committee also found evidence of 'lack of support for lessees, of verbal agreements not honoured, and on occasion of downright bullying' by the pubcos.

The Committee concluded that lessees should have the right to be free of the tie and asked the Competition Commission to investigate:

> Nonetheless, we note that intervention can have unexpected consequences. The beer orders led to the emergence of the pubcos. Displacing pubcos without considering the market as a whole may put too much power in the hands of brewers and wholesalers. The position of local brewers operating a small tied estate also needs to be considered.[4]

Cartels: a permanent feature of the modern economy

Cartels, although they are often substantially about market control and the maintenance of profits, are almost invariably more complex than they appear. The simple assumption that firms are ganging up to exploit customers may be true at times, but it is not often the whole story. This is evidenced by the difficulty of instituting remedies. The trend towards concentration in industry after industry appears to be inexorable. That may well mean that competition requires state oversight if it is to remain in the public interest, but anyone who views cartels and cartel type practices as simply an evil to be stamped out, a mere persistent wickedness like burglary, is as naïve as the legendary King Canute. Competitive choice may be the very heart of market capitalism, but is very far from its early nineteenth century beginnings, when all firms were small.

Choice and the big lie

Selling people what they do not really want is the stock in trade of the salesman: you cannot afford that coat, you already have one, admittedly different in style, but this one suits you, and the winter is coming on, and there is only one left in your size. Although we may find it difficult to believe that the blandishments of sales staff were as sophisticated in the days before industrialisation and abundance, they were surely as fulsome, wheedling and mendacious. They were not, of course, supported by an advertising industry anything like as extensive, insistent and, particularly in Britain, entertaining, nor by the customers' capacity to spend, not only in respect of disposable income – what is not already spoken for in respect of essentials – but of reasonable expectations of increasing future spending power (an interesting phrase in the context). How dreary to have our money sitting in the bank when we could be having fun! This is part of consumer culture, but it is not the lie in question.

Cars

The real lie is to be found in more systematic bamboozling. Some organisations offer you everything except what you need. Motor car producers, for example, refused for years to design safety features into their vehicles, despite the increasing power and speed of the cars and the number of deaths and injuries caused. It was not until the consumer campaigner Ralph Nader exposed the exceptional risks posed by some American models in the early 1960s that a serious safety campaign began.[5] Manufacturers doggedly resisted seatbelts for many further years, despite clear evidence of the injuries that could be prevented by their use. In the meantime cars were designed to be eye-catching, shiny, brightly coloured and elaborately styled, and promoted as fun to drive. The manufacturers also promoted the idea that you would buy a new car every few years and began to offer financial packages to encourage this. They thereby carefully distracted the buyers from another feature of postwar cars: the earlier cars of the 1920s and 1930s were built much more solidly and lasted well, many of them surviving into the 1950s. The new ones were deliberately built of thin steel and cheap modern plastic, designed to rust and fall apart in five years, so necessitating replacement. Only the serious Swedes failed to conform, producing Volvos with extensive safety features and built to last. One might say (and manufacturers would certainly say) that nonetheless designs were later changed to improve safety and longevity, and that they did therefore respond to the demands of the public. In the case of safety this was not merely the demands of the public, but of governments.

Despite the health risks known for many years to be associated with lead, manufacturers claimed that engines that could run on lead-free petrol were too difficult and costly to develop and that, in any case, lead from petrol was an insignificant environmental contaminant.[6] Only when the playgrounds of schools on main roads were shown to be heavily polluted by lead from petrol fumes were manufacturers finally required by an embarrassed government to introduce lead-free combustion.

Car manufacturers are still at it. Modern cars are designed to protect passengers and to minimise injuries to pedestrians and occupants of other vehicles. They are still very bright and shiny, but of course they go out in all weathers and frequently have to squeeze into small parking places. It is surely odd that they are designed to show every scratch and dent. Anything but the slightest scuff will crack plastic, or dent metal panels, which are designed as extensive units, locked into the jigsaw puzzle of the modern car with special fittings. Much scratching of heads and sucking of teeth in car body repair shops is sustained by the manufacturers' art in designing repairs to be complicated and expensive, all in order to maintain a vehicle that is as vulnerable to damage as a child's balloon. Henry Ford was honest in telling his customers that they could have their cars in any colour they wanted as long as it was black. Postwar manufacturers have offered endless varieties of colour, model and specification, but have doggedly refused what was needed and wanted until compelled to do so.

Supermarkets

Another big lie is successfully perpetrated by the supermarkets. Like the car manufacturers, they have been immensely skilled in appealing to public weaknesses (we do not need cars, but they are much more indulgent than even a comprehensive and efficient public transport system). Supermarkets have made shopping easier: the butcher, the baker, the greengrocer, the fishmonger, the hardware shop and the newsagent and tobacconist are all under one roof, and the weekly shop can be done in one trip to the capacious car park. The products are laid out in a systematic order, with staff available to help, and the supermarket system largely eliminates counter queues by open shelves. Mountains of purchases are run through the tills at the checkout at astonishing speed with modern technology. All of this has been made possible by a formidably efficient distribution system, which replenishes shelves overnight. Economies of scale have enabled prices to be driven down, and vigorous competition has played a part here, though the advantage used by Tesco to topple Sainsbury's as the sector leader was not just price, but improved service. In their early years supermarkets became vast, dreary and increasingly inconvenient. The injection of a brighter, cleaner environment, a brisker atmosphere, a greater emphasis on service and staff trained to deliver it has transformed Tesco from Jack Cohen's downmarket 'pile 'em high and sell 'em cheap' to a store which appeals to a substantial majority.

Supermarkets have not achieved their current ascendancy by themselves, however. Behind them the food processing industry has been strenuously active. In the old grocers tinned goods were available from the nineteenth century. Supermarkets took advantage of freezing from the start. Frozen food has quite a good shelf life, although not as long as tins. As distribution improved, however, chilled food became possible, as long as it could be sold fast enough. So it was that supermarkets became the most comprehensive and sophisticated purveyors of processed food, and customers were sold convenience shopping. What customers were not told was that they were also being sold a loss of choice. On the contrary, they were being told that choice was ever expanding and this seemed to be evident in the brightly coloured packages on more and more aisles, and in the exotic food names: lasagne and chicken biriyani, as well as cauliflower cheese and shepherd's pie, and, of course, baked beans and spaghetti hoops. It would be unfair to say that these are all the same – some of the ingredients are different. They all, however, share common characteristics of which the public now complain: high sugar, salt and saturated fat content and high levels of additives such as monosodium glutamate, colourings, flavourings, antioxidants, emulsifiers and stabilisers. Products are tested by panels of tasters, so that the average, not the discriminating, palate is chosen. The outcome is twofold: first, everything is bland; and, secondly, a uniform palate is created, which expects and enjoys the sugar, salt, fats and additives cocktail.

To call this junk food is to miss the point. It may, in some cases, be pernicious and use poor ingredients. By offering apparent choice off the shelf, a generation has been systematically disabled from creating their own food choices and in the process many have lost the capacity to cook for themselves. The profitability of supermarkets and of the food processing industry is what has driven the entire operation. By the ruthless use of their purchasing power, supermarkets have driven down prices paid to producers. They have also insisted on the over-standardisation of produce, with the result that what is sold as fresh produce is what can be produced cheapest in quantity and heavily dosed with chemicals to eliminate blemishes and reduce losses from pests and diseases. This has resulted in the easier availability of vast quantities of meat, dairy products, all year round fruit and vegetables at very low prices, and with very little regard for flavour – blandness again. The blandness and lack of variation encourages customers to see the fresh produce for what it is: manufactured so that one item is exactly the same as the next. Discrimination among apples, pieces of meat, or cuts of cheese is thus irrelevant: you just buy the quantity and type you want. The blandness of the taste works nicely with the blandness of the processed food.

Herein lies the important synergy. Profit margins on fresh foods may be adequate, but the gross value is not high enough to be the basis for real billion pound profits. Processed food, however, commands much higher prices. The more customers can be persuaded to bias their shopping towards pizzas and shepherd's pie, rather than pork chops and bananas, the greater the profit. Research by the National Consumer Council found that, apart from Marks and Spencer, the major supermarkets were offering double or more the number of enticing special offers on processed than they were on fresh food. The drive for profit explains the vital alliance between the food processing industry and the supermarkets. Convenience shopping for convenience food has produced a feeling of choice, but the reality is that customers have been successfully guided in one direction.

Retail financial services

One might complain that, compared to retail financial services institutions – banks, insurers, mortgage lenders, brokers, credit card companies – car manufacturers and supermarkets could not hold a candle to them as liars. They lied to customers to sell personal pensions in the 1980s and 1990s; they lied to home buyers to get them to take out endowment mortgages from the 1980s until at least very recently; they engage in systematic deviousness over credit card rates and charges; they sold the elderly home income plans in the 1980s that left a good many at risk of having the homes they had already bought once at risk of repossession; they sold unsophisticated investors split capital trusts as secure, and precipice bonds which were 'sound', which in both cases suffered heavy losses.[7]

Payment protection insurance (PPI), which is supposed to help borrowers who get into difficulties maintaining payments on loans and credit because of illness or job loss, is also being exploited to boost profitability.[8] The wording of policies is designed to make claims more difficult than buyers of the protection would expect, policies have been sold to people who would be unable to claim anyway, and exclusions glossed over by sales staff. The cost of PPI can add significantly to the costs of loans and credit, yet they are not required to be included in the headline costs which are used to attract customers. They are then sold PPI either on the basis that it is prudent to have it, or, if the borrower's circumstances appear to the lender to be vulnerable, on a more or less compulsory basis. Like other abuses, the combined attention of consumer groups – in this case Citizens' Advice Bureaux – and the regulators – in this case the OFT, the Financial Services Authority (FSA) and the Competition Commission – will publicise the dangers, warn the public and restrict the industry's capacity to get away with it in time, at which point it will move on to the next wheeze.

These, however, are all specific faults for which, in a good many cases, compensation has been extracted thanks to progressively stricter regulation, first by the Securities and Investments Board, and now by the FSA, in recognition of the need for tougher action – the cost of pensions mis-selling abuses alone is in the region of £13 billion, with payments for endowment mortgage cases continuing. These are not the big lies. They are sometimes the lies of sales staff needing to earn commission and desperate to close a sale; sometimes the lies of management over-keen to promote a new product; the big lie is that still sustained by the entire industry. It is understandable, and it takes advantage of an open goal, but it is nasty nonetheless.

The real benefits which the retail financial services industry can offer are in practice quite simple: somewhere to put your salary and make payments for you reliably and efficiently; someone to lend you money for short-term borrowing; someone to lend you enough to buy your home; someone to cover major risks – burglary, car theft and serious damage, fire, death or disability; someone to look after your long-term and short-term savings. With the exception of risk insurance, these are not very complicated matters for the customer to understand, and terms offered could be simple: interest rates in respect of loans and savings, charges in respect of services. This is just the problem for the financial institutions. If they competed openly head-to-head it would be immediately obvious who offered the best deal. The solution has therefore been product differentiation, or 'bells and whistles' in trade jargon.

Time was when the building societies, as they then were (most are now banks and insurers), met every quarter as a group to decide on interest rates. They were guided in their views by the Bank of England, which directed banks as to what the base rate would be, and they made their decision as a binding collective, a cartel no less, but a legal one. This, of course, was anti-competitive, and was abolished as such in the 1980s, although mortgage lenders inevitably continue to be constrained by Bank of England base rates. Other deregulatory measures allowing demutualisation of building societies and their conversion into all-purpose rather than single purpose financial institutions sharply increased competition and produced a desperate scramble for market share in the 1980s and 1990s. The various mis-selling abuses were one outcome of these pressures, but the greatest problem lies with the deliberate obfuscation of product differentiation. Whose money is it which is given away so generously in a cashback mortgage? Whose interests are served by loan to value mortgages in excess of a hundred per cent? Which customers really understand the multiple options and the charges for them on their mortgages? Which bank provides a description of its interest rates and charges on current accounts in less than one page? The annual percentage rate was introduced by the OFT in the late 1970s to try to address confusion over interest rates. Few people understand what this means.

Money, in the abstract, for most people (accountants and bankers are obvious exceptions) is boring. Money is an instrument to enable you to do what you want – a means to an end. Making financial commitments complicated is therefore guaranteed to make most people's eyes glaze over in seconds. They are easy meat for glib sales staff and easy prey to headline figures offering apparently competitive rates, 'excellent terms' and 'security'. This means that financial institutions have found it far too easy to compete with one another, not on the real quality of what they are offering, but on speed of service – mortgage decisions in minutes, current accounts opened over the phone in half an hour; convenience – high street, phone, internet, direct mail, personal call; and the airy encouragement not to worry about money – we are on your side and our friendly customer services systems are always ready to assist. The close scrutiny that money should occasion, especially in medium- and long-term arrangements affecting a significant part of one's income, is deftly avoided. This is assisted by the financial illiteracy of the public. Education has been progressively modified to allow Shakespeare to be taught through film rather than a close reading of the text, but maths has not been adapted to teach the effect of compound interest on credit card bills, or the difference between an endowment and a repayment mortgage.

We shall have occasion to return to financial institutions in respect of credit below, but it bears saying at this point that the froth and buzz of service and simplicity and friendly advice with which retail financial services have surrounded themselves is part of the money illusion essential to a consumer society, a society in which getting on and making more choices is important, and money is, well, just money really, not really important, something you have to deal with from time to time, irritating as a constraint, but sooner or later there is more, and everything will be OK.

The object of the retail financial services industry is of course to take as much of your money from you as possible, so that they can invest it and make a profit whilst charging you for taking it from you. This is pretty good work if you can get it and the industry has promoted it with enormous success. It has found it only too easy to entice people with offers they not only do not understand, but do not care that they do not understand. The first big lie of retail financial services is hence that customers are genuinely being offered the choices that their advertising and promotion appear to offer; the second, articulated *sotto voce*, but very persuasively, is that money does not really matter that much. Everything will be fine; we will take care of it. This could not be further from the truth. No other industry has, of necessity, been so determinedly focused on margins and profitability.

Bad choices

A quite different kind of problem is posed by the social consequences of some choices, which in certain circumstances can almost lock people into cycles of choices, which end up disadvantaging most of them. Sometimes we may recognise such bad choices, but even then it may be difficult to resist them. It is important to note at the start that such cycles are not simply be to be explained by individuals being foolish or reckless, even though, with hindsight, they may appear so. In the situations they face the choices made may have been quite rational. There are a variety of examples which demonstrate that when the mechanisms of choice do not work due to human failing the consequences of this are not trivial and can impact in terrifyingly dangerous ways at both local and global levels.

There has been concern in Britain recently at the increasing numbers of young people carrying knives and, in more restricted circles, guns. The latter carry the very emotive connotations of power and status – 'respect' – in some criminal circles: producing a gun obtains others' instant attention and compliance in a way that almost nothing else does. In both cases, however, the fact that some people carry weapons, or are credibly believed to, and hence may threaten you, creates a dilemma: do I take the risk that they would use the weapon to threaten me to obtain more or less anything they want, including wanton mayhem or murder, or do I arm myself to establish a balance of threat? Many decide that outside help is likely to be too slow in coming in any likely confrontation, and choose to arm themselves too. The resultant spread of knives (and to a lesser extent, guns) progresses to their display, their threatened use, and on to their actual use. Police, schools and other agencies have hence been energetic in campaigning against weapons; penalties for possession have increased, and increased checks and searches undertaken.

Such arms races are by no means confined to the streets. Israel long ago decided that, having been persistently attacked by her Arab neighbours, a number of whom maintained a public policy that she had no right to exist, she should arm herself with the ultimate deterrent, nuclear weapons. Though still not formally acknowledged, Israel is widely believed to have had nuclear weapons for at least a quarter of a century. Not surprisingly, her neighbours, defeated decisively several times by Israel in wars, decided to follow suit. Israel destroyed Iraq's nuclear weapons development reactor in an air strike in 1982, without warning or explicit provocation. More recently India and Pakistan, bitter long-term rivals with inflammatory religious and territorial disputes and a history of armed conflict, have developed nuclear weapons and demonstrated their nuclear capacity within a short time of each other. This left Iran with nuclear capable states all around her, as well as vehement antagonism to the theocratic republic by the USA. Iran had also suffered huge casualties in a long war started by Iraq, in which nerve and mustard gas were used as well as conventional weapons. Iran, above all states, has reason to be fearful and yet it is one of the states that evokes greatest concern. Its president averred that Israel should be wiped off the map and it is run by a religious oligarchy who care far more about expectations of heavenly salvation than about human life, and which has developed and successfully exported the suicide bomber.

The Cold War, with its explicit strategy of 'mutually assured destruction', was a similar process of escalating nuclear armed choices, which it took exquisite diplomacy to contain and eventually dismantle. Robert McNamara, US Secretary of Defense at the time of the Cuban missile crisis in 1962, when asked how war was avoided replied: 'Luck', and that after he had paid tribute to the earnest desire of both sides and both leaders to avoid a war at all costs.[9]

Markets are subject to similar cycles of bad choices, which are rational at the time, but damaging in their outcomes. It is frequently assumed that the speculative bubbles that have afflicted stock markets ever since the South Sea bubble in 1714 are the result of a combination of greed and speculative fever. It is true that investors in bubbles do not take long enough to consider the real value and *bona fides* of what they are putting their money into and afterwards may feel very foolish, as well as destitute. Once a speculative bubble takes hold, however, more and more people will flock in and stock prices will rise dramatically. There is then a great deal of money to be made, providing you cash in soon enough, that is, before the inevitable crash. Where the boom is recognised to be speculative, caution is clearly the watchword, but there are the booms in which arguments are sustained that the price rises will be permanent.

The recent 'dot.com' boom was fuelled by the conviction, especially in the US, that the internet was a transformative technology, like steam, or electric power, or the coming of the motor car, that would drive industrialised economies forward in a rising surge, and permanently change business, with enhanced levels of efficiency, productivity and profits. Whilst there would clearly be unsuccessful dot.com companies, there would certainly be many that would be successful, just as the industrial giants founded in the nineteenth century and early twentieth centuries have become. It therefore made sense to get in as much and as early as possible when dot.com companies were floated, and it mattered not at all that all but a very few had histories of losses, not profits. Any scepticism was met with a vehemence of conviction that brooks no questioning, and which seems to be the forte of some Americans. In the event a lot of people lost a lot of money and it took time to recognise that the internet has its uses, but it is not transformative,[10] and that it is only certain operations such as eBay and Amazon which are uniquely suited to take advantage of it and so succeed spectacularly.

Speculative booms are not confined to the stock markets. Housing and commercial property are also subject to them and, in respect of housing problems, are especially difficult for potential participants. During the last major British boom in the late 1980s it was not just that ordinary, that is, not wealthy, citizens were buying and selling properties, because market activity was intense – properties often sold the day that they came on the market – and gains even over a few months were significant. Those wanting to own their own home were naturally alarmed to see prices spiralling upwards. Surely the sensible thing to do was to borrow to the limit before they were priced out of the market. That view was reasonable enough: historically house prices have very rarely fallen, although the rate of increase has varied widely, and values have generally stayed ahead of inflation. On this occasion, however, the Chancellor of the Exchequer finally stepped in to control the boom and reduce tax breaks for home ownership, and this was followed by rising interest rates and recession. As a result prices fell, many people were trapped in negative equity, with the size of their mortgages larger than the new value of their homes, and many could not maintain payments at higher interest rates and had their properties repossessed by lenders. The aspiration to make a lot of money from the stock market can be castigated as greedy. The aspiration to own your home cannot.

Credit and the money illusion

The rise of the credit industry has shadowed and enabled the rise of consumerism. From the introduction of hire purchase (the 'never-never') for consumer durables in the 1930s, to credit cards in the 1950s and personal loans in the 1960s (loans before then normally needed to be secured against assets as collateral), the credit industry played an important part in the rise of affluence. Mortgage lending for house purchases had been established since the nineteenth century as a significant institution, but only for the middle classes. As this group grew dramatically, not only numerically but as a proportion of the population, from the 1950s to the 1980s, home ownership secured on credit also spread, from less than a third to more than two thirds of households. Formal credit scores from specialised institutions, as opposed to an informal 'tick' from a local shopkeeper or publican, remained largely confined to mortgages, which were, in turn, a matter of careful calculation and advice from branch managers, delays whilst an acceptable deposit (five to ten per cent of purchase price usually) was saved up, and a wait in a queue for loan funds to become available. Even though mortgages were established as a credit institution well before the post-war flood, they were part of the culture of saving, which otherwise predominated. Who can now even recall saving up for a purchase, as opposed to simply going out and buying? Or having regard to one's current credit balance and perhaps calculating the rough cost of repayments if spread over various periods? Saving up used to be the only way to make large purchases, apart from borrowing from family and friends.

The growth in ownership of consumer durables – cars, washing machines and so on – led to a natural shift in appraisal. Buying a house on credit was sensible, because house prices tended to rise and houses were not liable to lose value with use – become worn out – provided reasonable maintenance was undertaken. Consumer durables do lose value, but their life is sufficiently long for them to retain significant value over the life of a reasonable loan, and hence to provide booty for the 'repo man' (repossession) in case of default.

Credit cards and personal loans, on the other hand, are entirely unsecured and have now become universal, along with charge and store cards and the instalment plans routinely offered to pay for everything from insurance to holidays to furniture, that is, credit offered as part of the sales package by the seller. The rapid growth of personal indebtedness in the past decade or two in Britain has now become notorious, yet the credit industry's appetite seems unbounded, with every opportunity taken to offer loans and credit cards on apparently competitive terms. Attitudes to lending have now reversed from the 1960s and earlier, when acquiring a credit facility was a matter of clearly demonstrating capacity to repay and proving a worthy need (overdrafts from banks had to be grovelled for): to borrow to buy a car, or for home improvements was acceptable; borrowing to fund a holiday bordered on the immoral, and was unacceptable. Now the slogan of one advertising campaign has been: 'don't put it off, put it on'. Money has been transformed from being something, always rather little, which you earned to keep body and soul together, to being just another consumer commodity to be shovelled out the door of credit companies as fast as they can sign up borrowers. And if you have too much credit, or too many loans, consolidate, roll up all your borrowing into one loan and cut the repayments by extending the term. If that does not work remortgage, and with a secured loan cut the interest rate. If that does not work, and you are still spending faster than you are repaying, go for an interest only mortgage, the term of which can be progressively lengthened so that you never pay off the loan and the mortgagor inherits the house.

Under the credit innovations of the affluent society of the 1950s and 1960s, therefore, money still mattered. Loans were *real money*, which you had to pay back, and therefore you had to be careful. In the credit frenzy since the 1980s money no longer really matters: it is mere numbers, numbers in a series of monthly statements, in bank accounts, in credit scores. Of course, if you are very silly, there is a different number – the one that comes up when you are in court – but that is not necessary for the vast majority. A bit of restraint for a while, a little ducking and diving and a word with a credit card company, a change of address, a sweet deal with the mortgage lender, an extra card with a zero interest credit transfer and you are away again. And you absolutely must not miss out on being first with that new computer game, taking advantage of that special holiday offer, making sure you have the lovely new wood flooring, not short for a night out with your friends for that special celebration. It almost sounds like lenders' advertising copy.

The real objective of the credit industry is, of course, to take as much as possible of everyone's money by lending as much as and more than they dare and charging a good rate for their loans, especially once the borrowers are in so deep that it is really hard for them to pay them off. If borrowers get into difficulties, there is a basis for imposing extra charges for administration, and increasing interest rates. One needs to recall the principal strategy of the loan shark – the one in the pub with the readies, who breaks your legs or your sister's face if you do not keep up repayments. It is not to coerce you to repay the loan; quite the contrary, it is to ensure that you never repay it, but keep on paying the instalments. For many in the consuming population the credit industry has now achieved this enviable position.

That, however, is not the greatest achievement of the great facilitator of ever increasing consumer choice, the funders of the economy. The real achievement is the transformation of money from something which is a tangible reflection of effort and earning power into something of no significance: just numbers, the numbers necessary to continue to have a good time, and sustain a way of life – to keep 'having a life'. Money does not really matter, it is a mere irritation, the necessary, no more, and therefore we should not bother about it more than once in a while.

Such a transformation of culture is, of course, not complete. Britain still has people who will react by saying in shocked tones: 'but I know exactly what I earn and what I spend, and I would never dream of not managing my money carefully'. Sadly, whereas at one time the reaction to this sentiment was likely to be either: 'And quite right too', or glumly, 'Would that I had been as careful', it is now likely to be: 'How boring! Get a life!' There are, of course, many more who see their work more positively, and view their financial careers more cautiously. They will, however, be aware of the insistent and incessant pressures to spend and borrow with which they live.

It may be tempting to suggest that, with the financial crisis and ensuing recession, all has changed, and that a more cautious and realistic approach to finance and consumption will emerge. We have yet to discover what lessons, if any, the banks and credit industry have learned, but the reaction of the world's leading countries is revealing. It has been to outdo the worst excesses of the banks in mobilising an avalanche of borrowed money to prop them up and to get them to return it to consumers in a desperate bid to keep everyone spending.

If people spend less they buy fewer products and services, and the producers of these goods cannot sell as much, so that they have to lay off workers, who therefore have less to spend. A downward spiral is created. The question of whether this strategy is right or wrong, either in principle or in its extent, is less the issue than what it tells us about the future. We must, it seems, get back to where we were with the least possible delay. It will take us a few years, and we need to curb the banks' excessive fascination with derivatives, but the way the system works is by spending, and that has to be sustained and promoted by credit. Only that way can the economy return to normal, that is, relatively full employment and steady growth. The outcome of such growth has been a transformational increase in wealth and income, the distribution of which is argued about, but not the overall increase. This is to continue indefinitely, and credit is its engine. So credit may be presented differently in the future, and there will certainly be a period of caution on the part of credit suppliers, but in the medium term there is no alternative; at least no leading politician or economist has thought of one yet.

Choice and duty

It has been argued earlier that it is instructive to consider the opposites of choice in order thereby to see how society and culture has changed, and to better delineate the meaning of choice today. In the last chapter provision was presented as the institutional alternative to choice, with intermediaries emerging as a potential alternative, although they are better seen as a support for choice. The current power of choice, however, lies not just in its pervasiveness as an institution, but in its persuasiveness as an idea which dominates our thinking about how to manage our society and economy. 'Giving people the choice' is somehow always good, albeit unfettered choice may not always be the complete answer. Already the ideology creeps through. Choice is good because it is free – cast off those fetters. It conveys good news, it is affirming, empowering, even indulging and fun. There are choices, as we have seen, which are not like this, and in Part Two we will look more systematically at major complexes of choices which are often anguished. That, however, is reality, not ideology. What is the ideological opposite of choice? What would a society dominated by it feel like?

Clearly it would feel less free, more constrained, less indulgent, more serious. We are not talking about the logical opposite of being able to make choices, which is clearly not being able to do so, but the moral opposite in terms of the *meaning* of being able to do so. That opposite is duty. Duty does not prevent or rule out choice: indeed duty only arises when there is a choice, but it does constrain, as in the phrase: 'he had no choice but to do his duty'. Duty is very much about choices, but they may be demanding and, unless you are very lucky, they are not fun. Above all, duty concerns obligation to others, in direct opposition to self-interest. Its use has now become almost confined in its full sense to the armed services, the only major institution which formally celebrates duty as one of its central features.

A century ago duty was as much a cultural *leitmotif* as choice is today. Literature and the press constantly lauded it, and it had been hammered home endlessly in speeches, articles, essays and sermons, by worthy voluntary organisations like the boy scouts and the temperance movement, in sentimental poems about the noble commitment to duty of even young children and animals. The message was that society was held together, enabled to advance and secured by those who did their duty. It was weakened by those who selfishly thought only of themselves. It was this sense of duty which enabled the First World War to be fought, at least initially, by British volunteers rather than conscripts. (That, it may be said, is not necessarily a recommendation of duty: the massive death and maiming of that war was senseless.) A society less fascinated by choice as a central ideology would be more open to the moral connotations of duty. Whether that is desirable is a matter for debate.

Conclusion: spoiled for choice

This chapter has looked at some examples of the way choice has been extended, usually with the claim that it is an improvement. In conjunction with the two preceding chapters, on how we go about making choices, and about how choice came to be a leading feature

---

119

of our society, it has highlighted how choice does not always deliver what it claims. In particular, this chapter has shown choice to be at times abusive and disadvantageous, rather than a boon. That has been the purpose of the arguments and examples. To return to the beginning of this book, this is not to claim that choice is 'bad' rather than 'good', but rather that it is almost invariably presented as good, and more of it as advantageous: choice legitimises. The culture of choice which this sustains diverts attention from and de-legitimates alternative arrangements, notably provision, whilst simultaneously diverting attention from providers, since no one has to settle for what is offered: there is a choice and responsibility for it lies with the chooser. Further it diverts attention from speciousness, lies and abuses by focusing attention on the benefits of providing a choice. This is not to claim that all the extension of choice provided by the consumer society is problematic or abusive. Most of us can cope with more extended choice most of the time. It is to claim that some of the abuses attendant on and created by extended choice are seriously damaging, that in some serious instances more choice is not progress, and that a much greater degree of scepticism about choice is necessary.

We have not, however, reached the end of the potential for critique. In Part Two we will look at a series of choices which have been generated by the same set of social changes that produced the consumer society, but which are demanding, intractable and sometimes insoluble, as well as new. These are not easy choices, nor always obviously beneficial ones, but we are landed with them.

Part Two

Choice and the life cycle

SIX

Introduction: choice and the life cycle

Our lives are marked and structured by major features that determine who we are and how we live. Still the most important is where we are born, socially and geographically. This provides us with the elements of an identity, national, regional and in terms of social class position, religion and political and social outlook, childhood security and, thence, education. These inherited features can now be more easily challenged, modified or discarded, although they remain, for most, powerful influences throughout our lives – the social class position you were born into, for example, remains the best predictor of the position you will end up in, despite the considerable class mobility of the past two generations.[1]

Once we reach adulthood, however, where we attempt to go socially and economically, as well as physically, is substantially down to us as individuals. Decreasingly little is available by way of guidance in the major choices we make in our lives: which occupation or career to pursue; who to ally with in a primary relationship, to have as a partner or spouse; when, how and with whom to have children; how to manage retirement, both financially and in respect of the use of time; and how to deal with the prospect of infirmity and our final demise. For some, health too is a continuing preoccupation, but those for whom it is a necessary one before old age are in a minority, whereas all the other issues must be addressed by us all at some point.

Or must they? Don't many people just rub along, as they always have, in an undemanding way, see what life throws at them and try to make the best of it? This certainly used to be the pattern only a few generations ago. Job choice was strongly influenced by family and location; spouses were, if not from next door, from the locality (seen in the social sense of a social network based on work, family, neighbourhood and recreation), and spouses were spouses, not partners and lovers of varying degrees of seriousness. Children were a natural consequence of marriage for most and an often sad absence for some. Retirement was brief, and exhaustion, poverty, industrial diseases and poor housing claimed many quite quickly. Life expectancy beyond sixty was, for most, much nearer ten years than thirty.

We have emerged over the past two generations since 1945 from a period in which we increasingly could make choices in each of these areas, into one in which nearly all of us expect to. Health has improved and life expectancy extended significantly, so that people can anticipate what has come to be called 'the third age'.[2] Birth control has become reliable and widely accessible, which has allowed those who want to do so to plan their children's births. Restraint on who we marry and, latterly, if we marry and if we stay married, or whether we pursue other relationships, has progressively declined and has now more or less collapsed. Jobs have ceased to be an inevitability in terms of available work, educational attainment and family tradition, to become much more a matter of individual choice. During this period of change it has been possible for at least some to continue to let things happen and follow obvious paths. To do so now would be to risk being thought feckless, and such a view of life is associated with the poor, whose lives are still highly constrained and uncertain, and who are compelled, as ever, to think in the short term, even when they might like to think in the longer.

For the great majority, jobs, partners, fertility, retirement and infirmity now involve inescapable choices. Although elements of reversibility have entered into all but the last, the significance of the issues around each of these is recognised as substantial, and the decisions in respect of them are highly individualised. We can seek advice from friends and family, as well as specialised sources, and we often obtain support for our decisions, and support when things go seriously wrong, as they do for many. In the end, however, the choices are ours as individuals. Nor would most of us have them otherwise: having someone else tell you which job to take, which partner to settle with, when and if to have children, for example, is now seen as an outrageous imposition. It is outrageous because it conflicts with the ambition that underpins the commitment of most to individualistic choice in life-determining decisions, and to a strictly limited role for parental and other guidance: self-fulfilment.

Identifying quite what this means is not easy, but at least part of it concerns self-realisation, that is, a notion that who one is can only be discovered and achieved by the careful, and at times experimental, pursuit of options that develop talents, and which accommodates to and takes advantage of the strengths of one's personality. The latter suggests the links with the shorthand account of this aspiration for many: happiness. The underlying rationale is that only by finding out what you are really good at, and what fully satisfies you, will you be able to develop yourself to the full, to get the most satisfaction out of your work and your life, and to contribute most to society.[3] Similar arguments apply to the pursuit of the right partner, the location of whom will not only give you emotional security and fulfilment, but provide a basis for procreation. Get these right and your life, even in the unforeseen adversities it throws up, will be a doddle. Get them persistently wrong (and most need several attempts), and you will be a mess.

There is some caricature here, and more detailed discussion must be delayed until the five life cycle issues are considered individually. What should be clear is the contrast with the opposite view, where tradition and duty prevailed. You take the job your father did because it is good work, respectable and that is the family tradition. You marry who your parents approve, even if they do not select your partner, because not to do so would be unthinkable, insulting and damaging to the family, not to say probably a disastrous marriage. Children follow naturally, God willing. Old age comes to those who survive, and younger generations should care for the older. Although families from more traditional societies may sustain a respect for these familial duties, it is generally only in respect of children that any developed sense of duty survives today. For the most part, the only way in which duty could be accommodated is duty to self. Sustaining oneself as an effectively functioning social being is a full-time preoccupation.

Vital choices in the life cycle are hence seen as the key to fulfilment and self realisation: choice is good news and celebrates the absence of constraint. Nonetheless, the choices involved are far from easy to get right, and there is a constant feeling of comparison with others who seem to have done better, as well as comfort from those who have done worse.[4] These vital choices are no longer optional. The opportunity costs of ignoring them and just drifting are now critical, although, as we shall see, putting some of them off has become a useful tactic, and even a significant social institution. Why, to sum up, are these choices now compulsory?

- Because the old constraints on them have gone, as discussed above.
- Because there are no default solutions: the system cannot be relied upon to make an acceptable decision for you.
- Because, as indicated above, we are taught to want satisfaction from our lives, not mere survival, to demand what we want rather than to accept what happens.
- Because these issues are about us as individuals par excellence. No one else can know us like we do. Others can advise, but in the end we have to make a judgement about ourselves and our opportunities and seize them – or, even better, create them.
- Because change is constant and previous generations are therefore unable to accumulate knowledge that is any real guide to the new one and the distribution of wisdom is, sadly, rather random. Futures, lifestyles, expectations, resources, problems and options change. Besides constantly changing occupational opportunities and uncertain limits on all of them, the present generation has to deal with gay as well as heterosexual relationships as an option for men and women, fractured families and their children, dramatic advances in medicine (although many seem to herald more than they deliver).
- Because knowledge is expanding at a ferocious rate and we can now do things we formerly could not, and the range of choices we face in respect of life cycle issues is larger and more complex, and here we really do need to 'maximise' and get it right.

Besides making these choices necessary, these factors also make them oppressive and bewildering, and ensure that we often remain uncertain about whether we have done the right thing, for ourselves or for others. Reversibility and delay offer comfort, not a solution, and the constant flood of ever more knowledge second guesses us. In these areas too, the confident chooser is at a limited advantage: they may be ecstatic about finding a wonderful job, or a perfect husband, only for things to turn out otherwise. At the same time, those who fail actively to pursue these issues are in danger of becoming increasingly isolated and of 'drifting'. Constant attempts to get the choices right preserve an often ephemeral sense of control – a sense that we have an identity and are going somewhere – a matter to which we will return in Part Three. The outcome is that choices in this area are necessary, very consequential, highly individualistic and uncertain. They may have their high points, but they also involve much anguish.

As well as being new choices with far reaching consequences these life cycle choices are, then, substantially ones we confront as individuals. Their modern characteristic is precisely that which has eliminated the elements of provision. People used to fall into jobs that lasted most of their lives and fall into marriages that were simply taken for granted. Some no doubt still do so, but are liable to criticism for not being more discriminating, ambitious and persistent. Similarly, children used to 'just happen' for some, and no doubt also still do, but at the price of being considered fecklessly irresponsible if the circumstances of the birth are undesirable: 'Why did you not think…?'

Whilst provision has been largely withdrawn, intermediaries have flourished, however: advice and support organisations, both state and voluntary, about all aspects of life, from expensive career guidance and life coaches, to introduction and dating agencies, to abortion and fertility clinics, besides the self-help and sufferers' groups that emerge so rapidly for those with a particular affliction or quandary, all greatly assisted these days by the internet. All these interventions and supports offer a means of mitigating the overwhelming oppressiveness of life cycle choices. The deal seems to be: you can mitigate the pressures and the anguish, you can benefit by being put in touch with others who are and have been going through it, but, in the end, it is you who has to make the choices, you have to do it by yourself. Such is the diversity of what is available by way of compensation and support that there will not be space to cover it all in the inevitably brief vignettes that follow. Their purpose is to identify the salient and difficult choices that we are faced with in the course of our lives, and to establish the point in each case that here is something both demanding and relatively new, the outcome of the last century, sometimes of the past half century. These choices are demanding but necessary, often very difficult to be sure you have got right and, in a good many cases, not reversible, sometimes not at all, in others not in any real sense that returns you to where you once were: fateful choices. Most have been struggled for as practical political rights and collectively almost define our modern condition, yet they often yield as much anguish as satisfaction. As such, they give choice a decidedly ambiguous rather than a benign character.

SEVEN

Jobs and careers

As a child I became familiar with the question: 'What do you want to be when you grow up young man?', and with the immediately acceptable, if jocular, answer that was often offered: 'An engine driver, I expect'. That was what all boys were assumed to aspire to (although I am afraid my reaction to the vast clanking mechanical wonders of the steam locomotive was, for a good many years, more fear and awe than any desire to control one). What is of most interest in the question today, however, is the unreflective use of the word 'be'. Intergenerational relations are now much less avuncular and more cautious: children's rights lurk everywhere. The most that I can imagine anyone asking today is a diffident: 'Do you have any idea what you might *do* when you grow up?' Yet work is still a powerful source of identity, perhaps the most important public element, along with age, after gender. The revelation of 'what he does' in a discussion of a third party still ensures an understanding, 'Ah', and a nod: occupational identity acts like a central piece in a jigsaw puzzle, enabling sense to be made of other fragmentary information. Occupations have cultures, some, like the police, medicine and the law, are very powerful and well known, others, like catering or painting and decorating, are less publicly pronounced, but nonetheless significant for participants. Fitting in at work has always involved adapting your personality to the workplace and the occupation and accepting that, over time, they will mould it.[1]

Work also involves making use of your talents, and a tension has always existed between the need to work to earn a living and the desire to work for self-realisation. At its strongest this is expressed in the idea of a vocation, or calling, originally to the spiritual and social ministry of the priesthood, but by analogy used far more widely, especially in respect of occupations with an overt service element, such as teaching, social work or medicine. To achieve a satisfactory career outcome the young person has to balance interest, talents, energy, personality, the need or desire to make more or less money, and willingness to compromise over any or all of these. The least demanding person will be concerned with none of them and simply take the first job available. The most demanding may spend years either pursuing a job or career to which they have been long committed, be it stand-up comic or judge, or years agonising over which is the best route for them.

Formal choice of work has long been open to a progressively enlarging majority of the population. The English peasantry was never tied to the manorial land and its lord in the way that, say, the Russian serfs were, but the restrictions on their leaving it were considerable, legal, customary and practical. With the coming of modernity these restraints fell away, but that still left the restrictions of status and birth, as well as money, along with the religious disabilities disqualifying all but members of the Church of England from many positions, and in particular from public office, paid and unpaid. These were gradually dismantled with the spread of electoral democracy, so that by the end of the nineteenth century formal barriers to work choice (money and status remained powerful in practice) were largely confined to gender. That barrier was not removed until the latter half of the twentieth century, and informal and practical obstacles still exist.

Even if our formal choice of work has widened progressively over a long period, practice for most was until recent years powerfully guided. Parental tradition, following your father's footsteps, was crucial to many. Where this involved going into the same trade or profession, the familiarisation as a child with what the work involved, the hours, the skills, the stresses, the kind of personality which was needed to succeed, was a preparation, a pre-socialisation. Fathers and other relatives also played an important part as sponsors, vouching for the honesty, good time-keeping, capacity for hard work and ability to accept direction, application and 'character', as it used to be called, of the novice. Employers would be much more inclined to accept someone who had a steady relative to speak for them. Whether the work entered into was the response to clear aspiration, or a choice brutally limited by what was available locally – in the stereotype, pit or mill – occupational choice was, until relatively recently, highly structured: by location and the work available, by social class and the expectations that went with it, and by parental and family example, knowledge, guidance and support. You could do what you wanted, but that would make you different, cut you off from where you had come from and those who had nurtured you. As late as the 1950s, the generation of writers who became known as the 'angry young men'[2] were berating the snobbery of class attitudes that prevented the rise of ambitious young people and the resentment of working-class communities towards those who rose above their station and 'gave themselves airs and graces'.

Even up to the post-war period, change in occupations, although endemic in the industrialised world, was not, in most cases, sudden. Most occupations had a history and were keen to celebrate their respective merits and mourn the passing of former circumstances: the transition from steam to diesel locomotives, the move from private medicine to the NHS, the decline of grammar schools and the rise of comprehensives. Such lamentations – 'It's not what it was in my young days' – took place within a powerful assumption that the job itself would continue as it always had done: how would society and the economy exist without policemen pounding the beat, dockers loading and unloading ships, and miners digging coal? Children hence grew up with gradually broadening horizons of what work meant. The most extensive knowledge was of what their parents and relatives did, and beyond that the work of family and friends, or of the work they experienced in the locality: teachers, postmen, bus drivers and conductors, train guards and porters, hairdressers, bricklayers, librarians. Beyond them lay the penumbra of the more or less significant, but only vaguely understood: politicians, judges, the army (unless you had a relative in it), big businessmen, film and pop stars; and then the masses of people you knew about in a usually abstract way, but cared about little unless you had them in your family: taxmen, bankers, civil servants. This occupational world could be explored, and there were routes past the class barriers for some, but work was a reasonably stable world. Choice of work for many might be more a question of where you 'ended up' (hopefully not in a 'dead-end job'), rather than much in the way of calculated decision making, but there was plenty of practical guidance in the process and the practical rewards in the end were known, located and accepted. With the post-war boom of the 1950s and the establishment of an international economy dominated by giant firms and countries with ever-expanding state bureaucracies and public services, this vision of monolithic occupational stability was given more weight, all the more so given the prospect offered of an end to catastrophic unemployment.[3]

The social landscape of occupational choice has been transformed in the past two generations. Not only have entire occupations and the communities they generated all but vanished – dock work, mining, shipbuilding, the asbestos and tobacco manufacturing industries – but others have been changed almost beyond recognition – teaching, universities, secretarial work, publishing, the law, for example. Great expansions have taken place in financial services, retail distribution and warehousing, leisure and tourism, and computer-related work, and information technology has come to feature in almost every job, from the garage to the bank, from the lathe operator to the local government worker. A myriad of new occupations has flourished: events organiser, call centre worker, medical writer, public relations officer, genetic testing laboratory worker, door supervisor (formerly bouncer), mobile phone salesman, compliance officer, community support officer, business risk analyst, tree manager.

Further, the sustaining of high levels of employment and a wide range of job opportunities from the individual's point of view has been accompanied by a regular insistence that rates of occupational change will not decrease. There are no more 'jobs for life', and all are enjoined to expect several careers, not one, with the implication not just that any employer or business may fail, as has always been the case in an industrialised market economy, but that entire occupations and skills can be expected to disappear by being made redundant, being outsourced abroad, or being reconfigured into another occupation.

The knowledge and nudges that used to manoeuvre so many into occupational destinations have hence been severely eroded. Parental, family and community experience of work is now far less a guide for the rising generation, and old sponsorship patterns have all but withered away. For the young person it is hard to know what is out there, to get a handle on the 'wonderful range of opportunities' for today's market entrants. Of course, a lucky few will have some of the same continuities with family and friends, and some others will have that vital inkling of what they want, and the confidence to pursue it. For the ordinary majority with no clear sense of direction the situation is bewildering. The range of options is so huge, and yet you cannot understand what is really involved in any of them without both an appreciation of their technical demands and an insight into their work world and their occupational culture. The former is possible, although very time consuming, but the latter much less available. Nor is there any real security in making a choice since, on the one hand, what is available now may not last and, on the other, what may really suit you may be only about to emerge, and only become fully available in another decade. You are therefore exhorted to be flexible, adaptable, responsive, good at working in groups, self-motivated, accepting of change, willing and able to learn – all noble characteristics no doubt, but with considerable drawbacks.

True, not everyone had the virtues and capacities that were demanded in the old world of work – steadiness, reliability, diligence, honesty, good time-keeping, loyalty, deference to authority – but something of them could be acquired with practice, even if against natural inclination. The current requirements are more demanding of those whose personality and capacities do not incline them in those directions. Indomitable cheerfulness and a willingness to learn, adapt and move on are qualities that have always served people well at work, along with a keen eye for self-preservation and the main chance. The expectations to accept change and be flexible today, however, require the worker to forgo the pleasures and security of sinking his or her identity into work and to become a chameleon. The loyalty that is fostered by and benefits from commitment to an occupation and to an organisation within it, and to those it serves, with growing experience and the recognition of what doing the job well really involves and requires, is now irrelevant. Those who remain in post for more than a few years are regarded with disdain. Move on, move out and move up becomes the necessary strategy. People who do not move for long periods are regarded as has-beens, while people who succeed spend shorter times in jobs the further they are likely to go up the system, seeing each as a stepping stone to future success.

This is made more pronounced by the rise of public relations, marketing and presentation as a feature of all work and work organisations. Public relations spin and the press releases, the corporate mission statements and ludicrously pretentious self-advertising of organisations (by no means just businesses) has its counterpart at the individual level in the CV as an art form, with its tactical lies and exaggerations, the 'blagged' interview, and concern with 'face' and 'coming across' as the path to success. 'Never knowingly undersold' is the cynical watchword of the successful modern worker.

The prelude to entry into work has, it might be argued, been further and further extended, to allow time for preparation for success in this demanding kaleidoscope. The length of compulsory education has been extended to the age of sixteen, and a firm expectation established that all should be in education or training until eighteen, with at least half continuing through higher education, and some of them going on to further postgraduate education and training. For those who do so in the form of professional or trade training a significant career path is plain, at least for the time being. For the majority who do not, extended education provides no access to the worlds of work beyond the pathetically limited 'work experience'. Education is academic and abstracted from the reality of work. Employers are insistent on public examination successes as a passport, even for considering people for jobs, whilst at the same time bemoaning the literacy and numeracy of those who have achieved them. Children reach adolescence in the knowledge that education is increasingly important, and yet what they learn in education gives them no insight into the work in which they might seek to spend at least part of their lives.

This amounts to a formally organised segregation of the young into a prework ghetto, a period of protected youth where they are maintained by parents and served by the state, and anxiously protected from the realities of the adult world of work. When they are finally precipitated into it at sixteen, eighteen or twenty-one, it is scarcely surprising that a good many do not treat the process seriously. How can they make reasonable decisions about what to do with themselves when they are presented with such a bewildering diversity with such a comprehensive lack of preparation and such a substantial absence of practical and relevant advice and information? Their solution is to take advantage of the options for work and do something which is available and which enables them to pick up a few useful skills and experience to go on a CV, but to continue to direct their energies to the continuation of the hedonism of a privileged age grade, youth. The great upside of work is income, and with income comes credit worthiness. Life is hence orientated to the leisure that can be chiselled from the demands of work, and is motivated by evenings in pubs and clubs, the weekends in specialist recreations and holidays in increasingly exotic locations. For many there is also a lifestyle structured round intermittent work, with extended periods of travel – a few months, a year, occasionally more – funded by cash flow restored by periods of work in high income economies en route. What begins with the gap year, explicitly organised in theory to address the lack of experience that the closed world of education imposes, becomes institutionalised into regular time-out, and in the process more honest in its hedonism: no longer even pretence of good works for poor people in the Third World.

For those who take the issues seriously and refuse the grasshopper solution, and who are not blessed with an identifiable sense of what they want to do, or a natural optimism and energy that leads them into successful experimentation until a solution is reached, the situation must indeed look challenging. Doing what you were best at in school is no recipe for satisfaction, even if it is a likely path to a job. Herein lies a further twist to the current dilemma. The very availability of work for anyone willing to apply themselves and perhaps to move from their home town, along with the elevated living standards and security and hence lack of desperation to find any job to survive, increases the salience of issues around work satisfaction and self-realisation. Why should I do a job in which I am bored, and where I am just made use of? But what is really me? The nasty dilemma is that there is no real way of knowing until you try, and yet, if you go down one avenue, you progressively close off others as you become excluded by age, are seen as inadequate because lacking relevant experience and acquire financial commitments. At the same time, refusing to commit and flitting from one short-term job to another is even more disastrous, since you are learning little of any long-term benefit, not discovering how you respond to serious occupational possibilities and, worst of all, you are getting older....

Ageism at work is rampant, and is scarcely surprising in a world in which retirement ages have fallen sharply, middle management and established expertise and knowledge in organisations have been ruthlessly purged in the downsizing efficiency drives of the 1980s and 1990s, and the emphasis upon freshness, quick learning and adaptability rather than experience, diligence and reliability is widespread. Coupled with much higher work rates and long hours, potential employees do not remain prime prospects in many occupations beyond their twenties or early thirties, and even successful ones can expect progressive relegation from the front-line by their forties. It would be surprising if the reaction of some to these pressures were not paralysis and depression, although of course such casualties will be much less evident than the grasshoppers who alternate work and play, and the stress beagles who smoke, drink, chatter and labour to succeed, constantly eyeing their friends and colleagues to check who is doing best and whether their career credibility is still intact.

EIGHT

Lovers, partners, spouses

It is striking how similar our habits in respect of one of the other major choices affecting our adult life have become to those in respect of work. There we saw a move to reversibility rather than commitment – no more jobs for life, lowered concern for job loyalty, a willingness to switch occupations and careers as well as jobs. There was also a concern to delay making serious job choices, initiated by the extended period of education and sustained during young adulthood by many in the desire to prolong a period of youthful hedonism, and in some cases to combine it with serious work in a work hard/play hard strategy. Finally, there was a concern with self-fulfilment through work, and an attempt to avoid work that was just a job with little personal meaning, although this must be balanced with a variable motivation to earn money. Money motivation is, for example, the conventional explanation for the rising tide of accountants, although it should be said that accountancy is more interesting at the upper levels, even if the requirements of audit are meticulous and tedious.

It is the element of fulfilment that is to the fore with marriage, with love and happiness being the primary and overridingly dominant objectives.[1] A good many no doubt still, as they always have, marry for financial security, but are derided as gold diggers or gigolos, tolerated much as prostitutes are, especially if skilled and glamorous. In the world in which women and men have equal access to education and training, and increasingly equal access to jobs (even if this is not fully achieved the expectation is well established), everyone is expected to make their way in the world on their own merits. This leaves partners as a matter of purely personal, individual choice.

As with work, this is not new, although the degree of emphasis upon it is greatly increased. With the exception of the sovereign who, after several hundred years of nastiness over religion, was legally required to marry a Protestant, everyone has long been formally free to marry whom they choose. In practice, as with work, substantial pressures and conventions, especially from family, have influenced that choice. Religion has long been a significant influence – Judaism, for instance, has been sustained by in-marriage, and fears have been expressed in recent years that secularisation and marriage outside the faith will ultimately dissolve the Jewish community. In respect of the Christian denominations, religion has declined for most to a nominal level and, hence, its influence on marriage remains primarily as a location for the service for those who want a church wedding.

As noted earlier, family, friends, neighbourhood and community – the people you lived with – formerly constituted the primary source of partners. Increased geographical and social mobility through education and work has meant that both locality and inherited networks, and the social class features that went with them, have been challenged for increasing numbers. As more young people move away from home and their home town, and up the social system and into new occupational worlds, the erstwhile natural, almost inevitable, processes of pairing up with those of similar backgrounds and outlooks has faded.

Other things have also had a dramatic impact. The institution of marriage has all but disintegrated. Even a church wedding with solemn vows of lifelong commitment before a priest can be followed in a few months by a civil divorce. No longer do couples 'have to get married', as they did up to the 1960s, because the woman is pregnant. Divorce has been progressively liberalised since 1948 and marriage is now no more than a civil contract, voidable at will by either party, with rules for the sharing of joint property in the aftermath, although more complicated when there are children, a matter to which we will come in the next section. Those who commit themselves 'until death do us part' may do so with the greatest seriousness and integrity, but the institution through which they do it perpetrates a social lie, since either can back off and try again (although not necessarily next time round through the auspices of all churches), whenever they want. For that reason many couples do not marry, even when they have children.

More significantly, there is now a complete spectrum of relationships involving sexual partners, from the one-off encounter to the piously and traditionally wed under religious auspices, who would never contemplate divorce. In between lie the serial marriers; the cohabiters, some successful, others less so; the couples with a stable relationship who are not cohabiting, whether as a prelude to doing so, perhaps because jobs, distance and money prevent it, or because, after divorce, they are reluctant to take the risks and endure the compromises of cohabitation again: 'living apart together' is now the choice of two million couples recent research by the ONS has discovered;[2] and the lovers, who may be more or less passionate, and have elaborate or no plans, and be at any stage in their lives. And let us not forget those who have simultaneous partners, whether known to one another on not, and whether also themselves other people's partners or not. And those in gay relationships, whether as part of a lifelong sexual orientation, or as a phase of exploration in a predominantly heterosexual one. Two generations ago this spectrum of sexual habits would have been seen, and was warned against, as utterly depraved. Its acceptance, indeed its celebration, is testimony to the extent to which individualistic choice is paramount today.

In the area of primary personal relationships and sexuality we tolerate no restraint or interference, and precious little advice. There is a stereotypical normative pattern, a convention only, that foresees experimental lovers in the teenage years being followed by progressively more serious relationships in the twenties, to cohabitation in the late twenties, and then to children and marriage in the early thirties. This 'Bridget Jones' progress is dictated by female fertility patterns and by the extended period of youthful hedonism (as discussed above), which seems to run out of steam by the mid-thirties. The Bridget Jones syndrome, based on failure to succeed in this process of mate attraction, and its considerable resonance with the younger population, is evidence of the failure of this normative pattern to deliver for considerable numbers, for whom panic and despair then ensue.

For them, and for the many more enduring the anguish and isolation of divorce and separation, introduction agencies and social clubs have become progressively widely established to provide semi-formal routes to finding new partners, in recognition that the wave of change has produced such social disruption that established patterns for identifying potential matches are no longer effective.

Family and friends may now be too distant, and most friends paired up; work relationships may be part of the fun and dare of youth, but can be hazardous, and may be officially frowned upon. And what do you do when life is no longer a constant round of clubs, parties and events? Suddenly people have domestic concerns and, whilst there are no doubt lots of you out there who do not, lifestyle becomes less conducive to bringing people together.

In this most personal of areas, in which the right of individual choice has been most insisted upon, it has turned out, for some at least, to be a challenging pressure. (It is peculiarly hard to tell how many of those who want to avoid single status may decide to convert an existing and more or less adequate relationship into marriage.) The acceptance and spread of introduction agencies, from the early marriage bureaux of the 1940s and 1950s, to the establishment of Dateline in the 1960s using basic computerised technology, to the rise of a range of increasingly professionalised full service introduction agencies in the 1970s and 1980s and, finally, the shift to internet-based agencies in the past decade, has mirrored the increasing individualisation of partner choice and the decline of traditional sources of support. Agencies now act as intermediaries providing support in the marriage and partner market.

But, you might complain, 'Surely you are describing a part of life in our society where people have been freed from past constraints to do exactly what they want? Are you suggesting a return to the system where people were nudged and manipulated into marriages, and found it almost impossible to escape them when they did not work?' Here, as elsewhere, I am attempting to describe and connect, and to identify problems. I agree it may be argued that we have a society in which, for the first time certainly for a very long period, everyone is free to follow their heart. But, I might reply, 'and a fine mess that has got many of us into', since for far too many following your heart means losing your judgement. Given the options of being more or less actively guided and advised, or of being free to look, explore, experiment and choose at will, most of us have demonstrated, by dismantling the restraints over the past two generations, that we would go firmly with the latter. The downside of the right to permanent experimentation, however, is not only a great deal of anguish and suffering and loneliness, but chronic uncertainty, which translates into insecurity. For the right to always be able to change one's mind about one's potentially lifelong partner means that one is always open to doubt and to alternatives. The danger is that the grass always looks greener on the far side of the hill. One becomes only too familiar with one's beloved's imperfections and it is only too easy to idealise the attractions and perfection, especially by detailed contrast (I am sure he is never irritable, she never has bad breath) of the only too accessible alternatives. The obvious weaknesses of unfettered choice are, first, that one may be mistakenly tempted by a new offer; secondly, that one may reject what one has at the first sign of trouble, rather than try to work through it on the basis of a serious commitment; thirdly, that serial relationships often have what are for most unpleasant periods of uncertain length in between them; and, finally, that refusal to settle fully (only ever until someone better turns up) may in the end lead to isolation. Worse, this may happen, not because you decided that after thirty years things really were not good enough, but because your partner did. It is, in other words, the institutional arrangements of choice in respect of marriage and partnering that is the issue, not individual behaviour, although of course that is not at all how it may seem to those involved in divorce and separation.

Again, you may complain, 'Are you really suggesting we return to a situation in which failed marriages cannot be dissolved?' No I am not. I am suggesting that the institutionalisation of reversible choice in a fairly radical form in place of a more or less irreversible marriage has disadvantages. I am also suggesting that the parallels with work are evident and the overall impact has been in markedly increased levels of individualisation, and of social disintegration and insecurity. It is these features that make these major choices in our lives hard ones, even though they are the ones we will probably want to insist on most: the right to choose our work and our partners. As with work, and perhaps even more so, there is very little guidance offered, at least of a substantial sort. There are endless self-help books on how to find a mate, and a good many on how to manage relationships successfully, and there are relationship therapists and counsellors, all testimony to the problems indicated above, and all relatively recent developments. What is lacking is any secure, unified message. As with partners, so with advice, you may look as widely as you wish and find wisdom where you will and where you can afford it. The same message that applies to partner choice of 'it seems good to me' applies also to the remedies when it all goes wrong.

This description is lacking in an obvious respect. It has so far skirted round the central feature of this area of life choice. Selecting a partner is seen as the central act in most people's lives that contributes to self-fulfilment. Get that right and almost everything else falls into place. Get it wrong, and, in the short term, life is likely to be unsatisfying and perhaps unpleasant at first with the 'bad' partner and then rudderless and lonely without one. True, some people opt out of the partner rat race at various ages and stages, but the vast majority do not, and even those who say they have done so would often be tempted if an appealing offer was in prospect. In a radically individualised society a partner is a bastion against loneliness and oblivion. There is therefore a great deal of pressure to persist, compete and succeed here, as at work, and there are considerable penalties for failure.

In contrast to the public world of work, however, fulfilment through partners is dramatically enhanced by the expectation of engagement at the most intimate and personal level, the most private of private spheres. While at work self presentation is a necessary skill, with a partner it is the real you that is available, and only if you can be yourself can real fulfilment and security ensue. This begs interesting questions to which we will return at the end of this book exploring what is the 'real you'. Crucially for present purposes, the question is comprehensively begged by the central institution in partner selection: love.

Love exists in many forms: love of friends, charitable (in the Christian sense) love for humanity, love for children by parents. It is romantic love that we are concerned with here, the falling in love that is taken as the touchstone that we have got it right, and the magical transformation that ensues when that love is reciprocated. Few people, incidentally, stop to reflect why it should be reciprocated, most taking the process for granted as a natural feature of our emotional make-up. The idea that it might be a mutually negotiated besottedness – a *folie à deux* – would after all demean it to a piece of silliness, which is just how lovers often appear to others. Love in the sense of fanatic infatuation, falling in love, does appear to be a cross-cultural phenomenon, at least as often seen as an obstacle to social orderliness as it is as a benign and desirable basis for marriage. Where there are, as in most societies, restrictions on whom you may marry and indications, if not prescriptions, as to whom you should, falling in love with a socially inappropriate person is bad news.

Our society has a rather sly take on infatuation. Most people recognise that it is possible to 'make a fool of oneself' with someone who was not really 'the one for you': holiday romances are a stock example. Most also say that 'really loving someone' is not the same as falling in love, in recognition that building a durable and worthwhile relationship takes further time, exploration and effort by both parties. Nearly everyone would accept that being 'in love' does not usually last and cannot be relied on by itself to sustain a relationship. Nonetheless, love is seen as the fundamental feature of relationships and the decline or collapse of it as a self-evident reason for ending a relationship: 'I just don't love you any more'. Some would also say that falling in love is the key test of whether this person is for you, although caution should be exercised. In the end, love in some rather unclear but substantially romantic emotional sense is seen as essential to the security and fulfilment that is natural and fundamental to human well-being, and (another problematic term) happiness. Further, the search for a partner is influenced by a powerful strand in popular mythology which claims that there is just one person out there who is perfectly suited to you. Find them and your troubles are over. This is a pernicious idea, since it constantly feeds the doubt about whether the person you are with is really 'the one' and fosters an unnecessary and destructive sense of romantic tragic doom: that many may go through life without this great consolation and that others may find it only fleetingly and be frustrated by circumstances (in the classic romantic literature because they are someone else's spouse, or because of geographical or status separation).

Rather few people, I suspect, see their feelings about the need or expectation for an ideal partner as the outcome of living in a highly individualised, free-choice society, with little in the way of emotional support once you have left your nuclear family of origin (which is why increasing numbers revert to it when things go wrong). With so few established and routine sources of dependable care, security and emotional commitment, and with such an emphasis upon the virtues and self-validating benefits of choice, it is scarcely surprising that we should invent a transformative emotional remedy in the form of romantic love. In a world in which change is a powerful expectation and where we are constantly required to adapt and 'move on', in which we can rely less and less on the past and cannot expect to know the future, finding a key other individual with whom we can ally and identify ourselves is a pretty obvious solution to the emotional demands imposed upon us. The really problematic part of it as a solution is the failure to recognise that it too is the outcome of those very same social developments. Love is a safe haven and a source of fulfilment when it works, but a very hard choice to get right, and very unpleasant when it does not work. In addition it carries a considerable danger of raising expectations about what is acceptable and realistic in relationships to levels that are unlikely to be attained in many cases and maintained in almost any but a lucky (and of course thereby iconic) few. To revert to the terminology introduced in Chapter Two, the pursuit of romantic love looks like satisficing: when we reach a recognised standard we stop searching. In practice, however, it tends to a lifelong maximising search for perfection, because the standard is set ever higher.

NINE

Fertility and family

The diversity of relationships, of sexual partnerships, and the requirement for constant choices between them and about whether to maintain them, is arguably an outcome of a commitment to personal fulfilment through intimate relations. It seems that we just find it difficult to get it right and have increasingly high expectations. Perhaps, then, the pains of perpetual choice here are worth the candle. With fertility, however, there can surely be no such toing and froing. You cannot get 'a little bit pregnant' and children introduce a third party, who is not only very dependent, but who had no part in the original act which created him or her.

There is a finality about having children that recent cultural shifts have re-emphasised. We now make more fuss about babies and children than we used to. Huge amounts are spent on toys and equipment and, in some cases, even vaster sums on designer clothes that the child will grow out of in weeks. We are obsessed with hazards to our children, whether in cars (those signs in the rear window), or in the playground, where children can no longer be packed off to play with other children without other adult supervision, or on the journey to school, which they cannot be allowed to walk or cycle alone, or from the risks of food, which has to be specially prepared and selected, or in anxieties about their progress and development, where a dozen books are consulted and intent concern turns to rapture at every normal achievement.

There are upsides to this. Few children are now available for adoption as babies, because 'unmarried mothers', as they used to be called, are no longer pressured to give them up. Levels of infant mortality have declined and health care improved, although at the price of the survival of numbers of children who, in the past, would have succumbed quite early to the frailties of infancy. Whilst remedial intervention can be dramatically successful in some cases such as heart defects and cleft palates (although, as the Bristol paediatric heart

scandal demonstrated, only if adequate standards are maintained[1]),
in other cases, babies survive, but in a very damaged and limited
state giving rise to all but impossible decisions as to who has the
right to withdraw life-support systems and whether it should be
exercised. Damaged, deformed and seriously disordered children can
be harrowing for the parents to cope with, and support services are
not always what they need to be, but these cases are a small minority.

For the majority of parents with perfect babies fertility has been
transformed in the past half century. Pregnancy is no longer a major
deterrent to sexual intercourse for pleasure. Not only are single
mothers largely accepted (the right-wing press apart) outside marriage
and long-term partnerships, they are not always readily distinguishable
from the casualties of divorce, with the result that single parent
households are now a significant and largely unstigmatised group.
The word 'bastard' is used as a term of abuse without reflection on
its meaning of fatherless child. At the same time, the large numbers
of fathers who have lost contact with their children and who fail to
contribute to their maintenance can hardly be considered a benefit
of the new order of family affairs.

Developments in fertility management between the 1960s and
1980s have given women substantial control for the first time over
when and whether to have a family.[2] Oral contraceptives have proved
widely effective and acceptable, and are supplemented by other
chemical and barrier methods. Fertility treatment for the sub-fertile
has improved dramatically, with the first *in vitro* fertilisation ('test
tube baby') now a woman in her twenties, and drug treatment to
stimulate fertility is now sophisticated. Abortion has been legal since
1967 as a means of last resort for those who need it, supplemented
by the morning after pill for those more alert to their mistakes. So
universal has control of fertility become that the boundaries have, in
practice, been extended to children, with a debate continuing over
the past twenty years, not about whether girls under sixteen should
have access to contraception and abortion, but about whether their
parents should be informed – a ticklish issue given that legally they
could only become pregnant through rape, since they are below
the age of consent, and parents are fully liable for their control and
welfare. Nonetheless, parents can be legally denied the right to be

told if their underage children seek abortion advice. Even when a child's right to privacy in the matter is outweighed by the risks to her, medical or other, the matter is to be dealt with through local child protection procedures.

Control over fertility has, however, led to an increasing tendency for women to delay having children into their thirties, when their fertility declines sharply.[3] Getting your relationship right by the end of your twenties is hence a vital step to being able to have your children before your mid-thirties. Leaving it later risks endless anguish, with increasingly invasive treatments and, of course, does not allow for the fact that your partner may be sub-fertile and treatment for men is less versatile. Research by the Institute for Public Policy Research shows that delaying having children has reduced births by about ninety thousand per year nationally.[4] A fifth of British women are childless by their late thirties, even though only five per cent do not want to have children. An aid to decision making has recently been offered in the form of a fertility test that can assess the number of eggs in the woman's ovaries compared to the expected average level for her age, allowing prediction of fertility over the coming two years.[5] This may offer greater precision in the management of individual fertility for women but, whilst it helps identify potential mothers, it does nothing to resolve the problem of who the father of the child is to be.

What the situation highlights is the dramatic reversal of the situation in which babies just 'happened', very largely to married couples. The determined and the sophisticated have always been able to prevent and terminate pregnancies, albeit often not without serious risks in respect of abortion (see the film *Vera Drake* for example). The majority have long been able to exercise some control over fertility: diversion (I have got a headache); restraint (we have enough children); barrier methods; withdrawal – all work to some extent and reduce the number of pregnancies, even if they are uncertain methods in the long term. Modern women and their partners have reliable control and therefore have choices to make about fertility, which, in practice, require a positive decision to have children.

This choice did not exist for most in the same full sense that it does today and it clearly interacts dramatically with partnership issues. The shame and sanctions upon pregnancy outside marriage in the past acted as a substantial deterrent. The absence of it, coupled with control of fertility, makes for very different and difficult choices. No longer do we live in a society in which more or less everyone gets married and the great majority of those who marry have children as part of the natural order of things, whilst not denying the attempts couples made to control their fertility within marriage. The decision to have a baby is now also a decision about a relationship, except in a few cases when a woman will choose to have a baby without a relationship. It is a major choice and, given the uncertainty of relationships, a major vote of confidence in each other on the part of the couple. But the fact that it is now a *choice*, rather than something simply to be accepted as part of marriage, raises further questions: do both parents really want children? Do they both want them now? Might the decision for or against drive a wedge between them? Will each of them be good parents? What does that mean anyway? Do they have the right to reproduce themselves? Does the world need another version of you? And are there not too many people in it already? At the same time children are a major source of personal fulfilment and emotional security, and are lavished with care and attention.

So, the decision to have children is a highly significant one and, once there is a child, it takes priority: children come first. Unless the relationship breaks down.... In which case it is the parents who come first, with one party leaving the household, a move perhaps over some distance, sometimes followed by a new partner with his or her children, and maybe more children from the new relationship. Now which children come first, exactly? If this seems too cynical a view, consider the issue posed by the parent who, after separation, finds new love with someone based a significant distance from the other parent. Should they take the child away with them, or leave him or her with the other parent and dramatically diminish contact? Or should they stay near their child and give up their new relationship? What do the children's views on all this count for, and how should they be assessed, notably as they grow older? An arrangement that gives at least some attention to the children's interests can only be achieved by sustained contact and negotiation between the separated parents, who are required to continue their relationship in order to continue to care jointly for their children, despite the fact that, in the absence of children, they might want nothing more to do with each other. Into this fraught situation issues of maintenance, care, contact arrangements, ever proliferating sets of relatives, friends and step-siblings, contribute to foment a heady and, at times, explosive brew. In many detailed instances in which choices need to be made and agreements negotiated there are no perfect solutions, nor evidently correct answers. To be sure, some parents manage it reasonably successfully, and children are very adaptable. And, it may be asked, is this any worse than the old system of maintaining appearances and avoiding divorce, or 'staying together for the sake of the children'? That is not quite the point here. The point is that our new system often involves both large and small choices which are very difficult, and benign outcomes are uncertain, despite our best efforts.

In respect of fertility, then, there are striking similarities with work and relationships, but also significant differences. Like those aspects of our lives, children are seen as a major source of personal fulfilment. Like them, because of the control we now have over fertility and the reduction of social constraints, the major choices involved can be delayed until the end of youth. Like them, there is a degree of reversibility, thanks to contraception, the morning after pill and abortion. However, all this has transformed what used to be largely accepted as more or less inevitable into what is now a major decision. Babies – or, for most, pregnancies of somewhere between twelve and twenty four weeks – are seen as irreversible. The consequences for those who get it wrong can be, as we saw above, ghastly and involve a long period of anguished choices. Even for those who succeed, further perils lurk: what should be the division of parental responsibilities? When should a mother return to work? Can full-time work be justified? Is it just financially essential? Can adequate child care be organised? What is the threshold of acceptability in terms of quality of care, time in care and the age of the child?

Child rearing

Once we have made the decision to have children and, for some of us, succeeded in the struggle to conceive and give birth, the question which overwhelms new parents is: how do we care for this tiny, largely helpless, new person? The support of families, although far from eliminated, has eroded significantly for most, and the declining size of families over the past century has reduced the experience of at least older children in caring for younger ones, and the memory of how things are done. The state and the voluntary sector have grown substantially to provide sequential support, from midwives, health visitors, clinics, National (formerly Natural) Childbirth Trust groups and many local voluntary and state-aided parent and child play groups. This flurry of support is dedicated to ensuring that the baby begins to grow successfully, that the parents can provide the necessary care and that the mother recovers physically and mentally from the birth.

After the drama of the early months, matters increasingly rest with the parents, with services – state and voluntary – available to degrees varying by locality, but sustained state intervention in abeyance until the start of compulsory schooling at five (although this is a matter being addressed by government in the provision of nursery places and other child care). As the child begins to develop and express itself, the issue for the parent becomes: how do we manage our child for the best? In traditional societies such matters are not the exclusive province of the parents, and neighbours, and especially kin, will not merely give advice, but expect to participate fully. Although grandparents can still be very helpful to some, we have moved a long way from a society in which they and other relatives might live in the same street and, at times, in the same house. In the past two generations we have reached a point where single parent families are common. Into this gap has marched a succession of successful authors on baby and child care, beginning with the redoubtable Dr Spock in the 1950s[6] and followed by a burgeoning range of others, many, such as Penelope Leach,[7] basing their expertise on the findings of the rapidly developing discipline of child and developmental psychology. These experts claim to be able to diagnose what the problem is when the child behaves in an unusual or problematic way, and address recurrent difficulties with sleeping, eating and potty training, grounded in an understanding of what human beings require from their parents in order to grow up as emotionally secure adults, capable of mature and effective relationships with others, and of making a successful contribution to society.

This situation is much more symptom than cure. Even with higher sales volumes and a further penetration of advice through magazines and radio and television broadcasts, the majority of the population will not be reached by such means. The principal benefit derived by those who are reached will be a slightly reassuring sense that there is a solution to difficulties and that there is no need for despair. Even though the reasons for children's aberrant or downright anti-social behaviour may be simple, they are often not evident to the untutored eye, still less the helplessly emotionally engaged parent. There is little substitute for the direct, on-the-scene advice of someone who has been there before and survived. Even though they too can get it wrong, child rearing is a practical skill learned *in situ*, and even harder to learn from owners' manuals than managing electronic equipment. Unlike electronic equipment, children cannot be unplugged whilst you attend to other pressing matters; they demand attention now, even if what you do makes matters worse.

The situation described here is essentially one of relative isolation – a problem that has become progressively more pronounced over the past few generations (although of course there are substantial variations between individuals and in family experience). Instead of child rearing being something rather taken for granted, that is, done the way it was done for you, it has become the source of profound uncertainty.[8] If this uncertainty were just the product of an absence of cultural input the problem would not be nearly as bad as it is. It would just be a matter of finding out the right way, or workable and reasonably effective ways, of managing things – following your instinct and common sense – and all would be well. These, of course, are just the words of comfort that advice manuals include along with their specific advice: you know your child, you care for it and want to do the best; what you decide is unlikely to ruin its life. Why therefore do we persist in worrying that it might?

Several additional factors impact menacingly on the situation and up the ante. The work of Sigmund Freud and his disciplinary descendants has now permeated our consciousness and become part of our culture. Its impact on child rearing was memorably summed up by Philip Larkin:

> They fuck you up, your mum and dad.
> They may not mean to, but they do.[9]

The previous certainty, based on a Victorian idea of the child as an unruly animal, whose passions could be tamed and whose full humanity could be achieved only by a sustained and firm upbringing, was replaced by one in which emotional violence perpetrated upon the child by the parent, perhaps as much by mistake or neglect as by crushing discipline, could cause irreparable damage to confidence, security and the child's capacity to function normally in social and emotional life. Yet of course children need a clear, reliable, supportive environment. How then to draw the boundaries between permissiveness and control? This difficulty has been made practically harder by the increasing necessity for both parents to work, and for the obvious pressure on single parents not to work: working mothers produced anxious latchkey kids, it was said.[10] At the same time, rising income levels and the increasing access of women to the whole of the labour force produced progressive increases in household income for many and the rise of affluence. The outcome has been high levels of anxiety about child rearing, extreme uncertainty about how to achieve desired outcomes, guilt about not being available enough to children in many cases, and about whether the right and adequate upbringing had been and was being provided.

The non-solution to these dilemmas has been increasingly obsessive child-centredness. Faced with fraught decisions about child rearing and the constant fear that they might be wrong, parents have naturally gravitated to a pattern that at least looked as though it would prove that they were trying. Child-centredness reflects a set of choices that parents feel incapable of making. The natural desire of parents to want the best for their children, the economic resources of affluence, the psychodynamically charged terror of damaging them and the absence of a clear, practically working model of what to do for the best have produced a kind of benign paralysis. Instead of a confident intervention and guidance the child is put in charge. The hideous consequences of what has been called 'paranoid parenting' are obvious. Despite their best efforts, the very anxieties of parents to do the best for their children transmit their sense of anxiety, not confidence, and the desire to provide what money can buy and to engage with children as equals for fear of oppressing them both generate a presumption of entitlement.

The crisis provoked by the dilemmas of bringing up children demonstrates, in an unpleasant way, that the choices with which we are faced, but which we nonetheless fail to make, still count and have consequences. 'I don't know what to do, but I will do everything I can' simply replicates confusion. It is a curious fact that the decline of duty in the wider world has been paralleled by the strong persistence of a sense of duty by parents to their children, but this is not returned in the other direction: filial piety is no longer the conventional morality it was a century ago. Despite the apparent swing away from permissiveness towards greater firmness and boundaries in very recent years, the dilemma of child rearing shows no signs of being seriously addressed since, as identified earlier, it is less the pattern that is accepted that is the issue than the security of the social underpinning. Within quite wide limits, various patterns and methods of child rearing probably work. What does not is a constant uncertainty about whether what has been done is right: the child is not equipped to provide an answer to that question, however benignly it is put.

TEN

Retirement

Retirement has recently become a pressing issue in respect of pensions, but the complexities surrounding the funding of old age beyond work should not distract us from considering wider issues about the retired as a social group that has grown substantially in recent generations and is projected to grow larger as a proportion of the population as people live longer. I will suggest below that the unclear and marginal status of this group, and the lack of clear expectations, recognition and rewards that should attend it in the way that they do other groups – children, youth, workers, parents, especially mothers – makes the retired a highly problematic social category. Hence, decisions about how to sustain oneself credibly as a retired person are challenging, at least for many.

Pensions do require comment, because pension provision dramatically affects what can be done in retirement: whether it becomes a poverty-stricken struggle for food and shelter, or whether you have a very wide range of choices available. The problem of the care and funding of the population beyond working age has long been dealt with by societies by some combination of savings, family support (as much practical as financial), charity and state provision. As in other aspects of welfare, the social democratic project introduced the state as underwriter and accepted individualisation of provision: families were not expected to provide, since poor people tend to have poor families and are therefore least able to do so. Although charities continued to provide supplementary support for some, they were recognised to have become incapable of delivering comprehensive provision. Savings thus became the primary route, with state subvention for those who could not save because they earned too little or too intermittently. By 1908, when the state pension was introduced, there had been more than a century of argument about entitlement.[1] The Poor Law system in its various incarnations never abandoned the concern that the 'undeserving poor' – those who did not save or did not work as much as they could have – should not benefit in relation to the 'deserving poor' – those who had been unlucky in suffering long periods of unemployment, illness, injury and expenditure on large families for example, but who had struggled as best they could, only to reach a point where they could work no longer, and with no savings. The object of the 1908 Act was to reward years of labour (most would have worked for more than fifty years by the time they reached seventy, the pensionable age under the Act), and to give the elderly the dignity they deserved, but to do so on a contributory basis, explicitly recognising each week of work. A distinction has remained ever since between the state pension, which is only paid in full on the basis of completed contributions, and welfare benefits targeted at older people, which are means tested. The main change has been the elimination of the moral element from means testing for all: eligibility is now based on what you have saved, not on whether you behaved prudently or recklessly in arriving at that position.

The objective of the state pension is to provide for basic living costs – it has a welfare basis. For state employees and the middle classes occupational schemes, based on contributions by employer and employee and supported by tax breaks by the state, expanded in the course of the twentieth century. These aimed at and succeeded in providing substantial pensions based on a proportion of final salary, usually a half or two thirds, allowing the employee to continue in retirement roughly the standard and way of life they had enjoyed during their working years. The schemes expanded progressively to cover more of the population as the economy came to be dominated by larger and larger firms and by an ever larger state; as the occupational structure shifted to white-collar work; and as high levels of unionisation, especially in large plants, allowed trades unions to negotiate participation for all workers in occupational schemes. Four problems have created a crisis in this emerging two-tier system, in which everyone gets a combination of the state pension and/or welfare benefits, and an increasing proportion of the population enjoy the benefits of an occupational scheme.

The first problem is posed by the success of the economy and increases in incomes. This has posed an increasingly pressing dilemma in respect of the state pension. Should it be geared to basic living costs, and if so how are these to be determined? Most would say today that it should include access to television and telephone, and anyone over seventy five gets a free TV licence. How much use of the phone should be assumed? Older people get reduced or free use of public transport, yet the public transport system is inadequate, especially in certain areas. Should it therefore include the costs of a car? How about a washing machine or a dishwasher? And holidays? To where? A fudged solution was to increase pensions from time to time, based on a calculated combination of rising standards of living, costs of living, what the government could afford and political expediency (what would appeal to the electorate). A solution was eventually achieved in the 1960s in linking annual rises in the state pension to rises in earnings, which meant that pensions reflected rising living standards. This link was, however, reversed by the new Right in the 1980s and substituted by a link with inflation, in order to keep costs down. Current targeting of means tested benefits for older people (with an inevitably elaborate form to fill in) has been claimed to have brought two million people out of poverty, but was challenged in the Turner report on pensions as creating a disincentive to save for many of the lower paid.[2] What would be the point of saving for any additional pension when what you can achieve would be only as much, or even less, than what you could expect in welfare benefits if you did nothing? Best spend the money and enjoy yourself while you can. The problem of the 'deserving' versus the 'undeserving' poor is still with us. Only when the idea of people living out sixty five years of calculated indolence in order to garner a few years of significant state support (they are not likely to be the healthiest group in the population) is recognised as grotesque are we likely finally to break free of this moralising obsession. Harry Enfield and Kathy Burke as Wayne and Waynetta Slob entertained us greatly and played adroitly to our prejudices but, issues of self-respect apart, how many of us would really want such a life of fecklessness? We derive satisfaction from making something of ourselves, and cigarettes, takeaways and TV are poor substitutes. But 'making something of yourself', as we saw in the section on work, is now very demanding and involves a long series of difficult choices. It is the Waynes and Waynettas who are likely to find them hardest of all.

The second source of difficulty also takes us back to the changing nature of work. The much greater flexibility now required of employees and the end of 'jobs for life' provided by big business and the state in the first quarter century following the Second World War has compromised occupational pension schemes. They depend upon employees contributing over a prolonged period in order to produce real benefits. Switching from one employer to another leaves either insignificant contributions frozen, to produce little at retirement, or the insoluble problems of transferring cash sums. Complexities here are linked to the other source of difficulty for occupational schemes, the fact that payments for pensioners are funded by a mix, which varies from scheme to scheme, of existing employees' and employers' contributions and the investment yields of the pooled contributions. For a long time high inflation rates and high stock market returns over the medium and long term have meant that occupational schemes were often successful in earning very large investment incomes. So successful were they in the 1980s that some employers took holidays from paying the contributions, and others seized surpluses that had accrued in pension schemes and ploughed them back into the business, thereby, directly or indirectly, applying them to the benefit of shareholders. This was challenged by various employee groups and trades unions, but such is the diversity of the way occupational schemes are set up that no general principles emerged from the courts. With the fall in inflation and a commitment by government to keeping it low, along with much lower stock market returns in recent years, occupational schemes have suffered a shortage of funds. Many schemes have closed to new employees and many more have shifted from final salary benefits to offering a cash lump sum dependent upon what the scheme can afford at the time the employee retires (although also dependent of course on employee and employer contributions). In sum, the occupational pension system is in disarray and there is now a widening gap with state employees' schemes which, since they are underwritten by the exchequer, remain in place. There is a clear need for some kind of compromise solution to produce substantial contribution-based benefits for workers, but in which they do not suffer as a result of regular changes in employment. How that is to be organised is the key policy issue.[3]

The third problem, which could be addressed by additional funding, both state and personal, has developed as women have become workers in their own right, and therefore not treated as dependants of their husbands and only eligible for joint and widows' pensions. In a society in which marriage breakdown and relationships without marriage are normal, but in which women still lose a number of working years through child rearing, restructuring is necessary. Current proposals are that women should simply be credited with state pension contributions during their work absences for childbearing and rearing, which still leaves gaps in their occupational scheme or a substitute. This might be addressed by a levy on those who do not bear children, but the acceptability of this is moot, to say the least. The likelihood is that, for the time being at least, women who have children will continue to suffer a reduction in final pension if they delay their return to work beyond a fairly limited period.

The final problem is the most challenging, not least because it is going to increase: longevity. Because people live longer, all pension schemes have to pay out far longer against contributions that are, in practice, reducing because people retire earlier. Early retirement can be compensated for by providing lesser or delayed pensions, but longevity requires increased contributions. This much is not in doubt. What is unclear is how such contributions are to be organised into schemes – state, private sector, or hybrid – which give good yields and are not liable to collapse because they are too small or too poorly managed, and which encourage workers to contribute.

The problem that emerges from the current policy crisis is therefore ensuring that everyone has a basic minimum and deciding what dignity and poverty mean, and then enabling those who can and do work to save effectively and ensuring they do. One route is compulsion: have one or a few large schemes and require everyone to contribute. For those workers who still have access to occupational schemes participation remains almost automatic and not reflected upon until near retirement, when consideration may be given to enhancing benefits by making additional contributions (buying extra years of service). Compulsory participation in a second pension would have the same effect and many support the idea but, of course, steps would have to be taken to ensure that the available schemes are secure and yield adequately. For the present, and perhaps for the indefinite future, the choices facing workers are unpalatable and impossible to make rationally. The example of Equitable Life is demonstration enough that even betting on companies with a good track record is not a solution. Measures have been put in place to try to prevent occupational schemes from collapsing, as a number have done in recent years but, twenty years after Robert Maxwell looted £400 million from the Mirror Group pension fund in a vain attempt to prop up his business empire, security has not been demonstrated, despite yet more recent policy initiatives.

So where should a worker put his or her savings? One disadvantage of not putting it in an approved pension scheme is that tax exemption on contributions is lost, but other matters may be more pressing. Paying off student debt is now a major concern of the third or more of young people who enter the workforce after graduation. Affording a home of their own is the next priority. Arguably the rate of return on it will outstrip most savings and pension schemes and, in many cases, there is an argument for mobilising all available resources to get into the property market before rising prices make it completely inaccessible. The requirement to be flexible implies a willingness to accept gaps between employment, which may require savings to fund, and retraining to move to jobs with better prospects and pay. Employers may provide that, but investing in yourself through acquiring skills and qualifications may also be well worth it. These financial demands are likely to take many people well into their thirties and career changes may continue well beyond that. Did anyone mention children and their costs in an economy premised upon two people working to maintain a household?

Yet, as all the experts correctly remind us, the earlier you start saving for retirement, the less you have to save, because of the effect of compound interest. Leave it until your forties and the proportion that you will need to put aside, even of a larger income, will be crippling. All of this points to a completely different savings strategy from monthly pension contributions from an early age. If income, including bonuses and pay rises, is likely to fluctuate considerably over a working life rather than, as under the old order, rise steadily to a peak and decline little if at all before retirement, maybe it is more sensible to think much more widely about long-term financial security. Major cash increases could be diverted at least in part into investment and calculated decisions taken over the long term on investment income, something many have started to do by buying properties to let, both at home and abroad, and by buying second, holiday homes. Many who have invested money in rental properties financed by buy-to-let mortgages have come to grief in the recent recession and banking crisis, however. Running or investing in businesses in your spare time, both legal and in the black economy, can be lucrative, although they are high risk. None of the options is secure or self-evident, none is susceptible to fully informed rational decision-making, and all have a large element of conjecture, ingenuity, opportunism and hard graft attached if they are to work. In that they arguably reflect the nature of the economy. Such a strategy means, of course, that there will be big winners and substantial losers. It also means that workers will need to remain open minded about opportunities and willing to seize them, be less scrupulous about how money is to be made and at the same time be willing to see their financial lives as a whole from a reasonably early stage and plan their initiatives accordingly, so trying to make their own luck. This description has echoes of what it takes to succeed in business, and history suggests that most people are disinclined to try to operate like this, because they are not made that way.

Establishing saving schemes for retirement to achieve for each citizen a financial basis for a secure old age and the chance of some comfort for most who contribute more because they earn more should not be beyond the wit of governments running current industrialised economies. It will require determination and skill to ensure the long-term commitment to the necessary funding, wherever it comes from – that is what governments are for. In the meantime all that is certain is that outcomes for citizens will be extremely variable and increasingly uncertain.

Those financial outcomes provide the basis for discussion of retirement itself. Where those outcomes are unfavourable it will consist, as it has for many centuries, of poverty and a constant, and probably gradually losing, battle to survive. Retirement will be taken up by constrained routines designed to minimise costs – limited travel and entertainment, skimping on heating, food, furnishings and clothes, and a proportionately constrained social life – a conclusion confirmed by Age Concern research on some of the two million pensioners still living below the official poverty line.[4] Health and ingenuity enable these constraints to be pushed considerably, but ingenuity is not equally distributed, nor is health, with the poor having the worst of it. In any case health will not last for almost all of us. Affluence has, however, created a growing group who will have something beyond the bare essentials, and for them a new set of problems is being posed.

Increased longevity and the ability of increasing numbers to retire earlier have created a substantial and very uncertain 'third age'. Unlike the transition from child to adulthood, entry into it is not greatly extended and adapted, at least for most, but arrives at retirement. More like motherhood, it is an anticipated, but still a sudden and often perplexing, even overwhelming, transformation. I do not know whether there is a retirement equivalent of post-natal depression, but it would not be surprising. Unlike motherhood it offers neither exit when children grow up, nor the compensating rewards of child-centredness. It is rather more like adolescence backwards. Where the young acquire strengths, skills, money and status, and the prospect of more in the future, the retiring lose them, with the prospect of less in the future, with the possible exception of money. Retirement is defined by what you no longer are, and its very existence betokens an ambiguous having worked one's passage on the one hand, and having exhausted one's capacity on the other. It also betokens a decline of competence and capacity that may not be immediate or automatic, but which is certain and one way – the only issues being how fast and what capacities, physical, mental, social and economic will fail rapidly or catastrophically. To put the matter more radically, the extraordinarily lucky or successful may retire at forty into a life of leisure. Those who do so in their fifties and sixties may initially entertain the life of a gentleman or woman of leisure, but increasingly face that of a geriatric existence progressively dominated by an increasing variety of failings. Health, mental and physical, is hence a critical issue at least as important as income in retirement, not least because good health enables those who need or want to do so to reverse retirement, at least temporarily, into work.

A normative ideal is emerging, which seems to address this, of progressive retirement. This involves a career with more demanding and highly rewarded jobs, peaking in the forties or early fifties, and then scaling down, with less demanding jobs, to retirement from full-time to part-time work in the fifties or sixties and, finally, pensions, skills and health permitting, from paid to voluntary work, allowing a run through the seventies. This ideal will work best, however, for the lively, open-minded, skilled, and those with good contacts and marketable skills. To ordinary mortals retirement precipitates a nastier version of the work crisis of early adulthood. It is not just the substantial loss of those work routines which pre-empted choices, so that almost everything in your day is now a matter of choice, but the lack of established objectives and constraints to drive you. All activities suddenly become 'hobbies', most of them very short lived in their justification beyond simple pleasure. The question 'What can I or should I do?' is now limited for many by energy and health as well as by skills and talents and, paradoxically, insofar as finance does not press, the big issue is: 'Why should I do anything?' Becoming an alcohol- and sun-soaked vegetable on the Costas, ultimately done in by the limitations of the Spanish health system, is one idyll, but no real solution.

Retirement for most demands a complex, shifting array of choices about identity and life management which did not exist when retirement was seen as no more than an implicitly limited period of well earned rest. The one thing on which the experts all concur is that the 'pipe and slippers' response is fatally sclerotic: you must keep active. This is the key question that the newly retired are asked by those yet to do so, and especially keenly by those approaching retirement: 'So what are you doing now, exactly?' Hence, I suspect, the many who take refuge in references to leisure such as 'Reducing my golf handicap', because it cues the response: 'Lucky sod', or who refer to continuing work – consultancy, home extension, jobs for the neighbours – because it similarly cues a reply implying legitimacy:

'Still making yourself useful then'. The more defiant may give answers along the lines of: 'Mountain biking across Alaska', or 'Travelling the world on our remortgage'. That message may impress some, but the sense of a breathless rush to get it all in before your health and strength leave you is unmistakable.

The fact is that there are no approved or socially accredited pathways in retirement, at least in part just because of those health and strength issues. We have made the transition from a society in which many did not reach retirement age, and most that did survived only a few years, to one in which most people have a significant period in retirement, but one in which capacity remains uncertain. What is required of the retired is not only a major reorientation comparable to that required of young adults entering the world of work, but also a constant adjustment in the light of progressive incapacity. Considerable skill, open-mindedness and tenacity are required to continue to succeed, particularly in the light of a perpetual flow of actual or implied comments along the lines of: 'Oh you're still doing [able to do] that are you? That's wonderful', and to others 'Of course he/she is wonderful for his/her age'. There is almost no escape from the progression to a status of being patronised and increasingly treated like a child, in the expectation that sooner or later one will become as dependent as a child.

Part of this comes from entrenched ageism. Older people are not elders with real power, they are has-beens, even if they are affluent; the very fact that they are no longer making their way in the world identifies them as non-participants. Practical age discrimination is now increasingly recognised and will need to be addressed as the population skews to the older, partly because longer years at work, part time and full time, will become inevitable, and partly because the old still have a vote and exercise it more often than the young. The emergence of a genuinely valued status group centred on the retired is very far off, however. The elderly are boring, irrelevant, conservative, a drag, possibly good for a few bob at times and when they (at last) die. They are not a source of knowledge (all outdated), wisdom (what?), power, or status. Respect: yes, from family and often intimates at times, but this is much more private than public.

The choices are insistent, substantial and far from easy. The outcome in many cases is drift, and this is permitted and accepted, and simply reinforces the irrelevance of the retired: the very word means that they are not doing anything any more. Being up and doing is the solution for individuals, but it is one that requires content, and it is that which is not readily available or, where devised, necessarily sustainable. Only when the retired are fully recognised as a substantial status group with taken for granted longevity and re-incorporated into the social mainstream will these issues really decrease. Until then, retirement as a social institution is still mainly the ante-room to death. The young are our future, bless 'em; mothers are the guarantee of our future; workers keep us all alive. The old used to be the pathetic residue to whom we felt grateful for contributing, many of them in war as well as work, and who would not, after all, last much longer. Now the retired are too sizeable a group, living too long, for us to be officially grateful. Instead they are just officially useless.

ELEVEN

Death

I t might seem fanciful to the point of contradiction to suggest that we might choose our own death. Surely death is the one thing over which we do not have control; the one great irreversible in our lives that we only get one go at. If we were magically to be given the option of choosing, surely we would choose to put it off? Near death experiences apart, it is certainly true that death is a one-way trip. The very fact that Jesus was supposed to be able to reverse it is taken to be final proof of his non-human character: only God can resurrect the dead.

This belief that God grants us life, gives us the freedom to live it for good or ill, and finally takes it away has been an influential theme in Christian culture, giving emphasis to what we still call the 'sanctity' of life. It feeds into our respect for individuals – all equal in the sight of God, and their equal right to life, and so into sentiments that lie behind democracy. If everyone, whatever their circumstances, has a right to life, then no one and no institution has the right to terminate a life. More widely it can be argued that no one has the right to neglect or abuse anyone in a way which brings their death nearer, or puts their life at risk. It is these lines of argument that have led to some contemporary Christians arguing strongly against euthanasia and abortion, although, interestingly, having less difficulty with capital punishment and war.

Niceties and varieties of Christian religious doctrine aside, what has been important has been the interaction of concern with individual life with advances in medicine and public health, which have progressively eliminated many of the causes of early death, whether from epidemic diseases or from the indirect effects of malnutrition and poor living and working conditions. We are now constantly upbraided about the consequences of our lifestyles in putting ourselves at risk: too much sun exposure, junk food, lack of exercise, alcohol, smoking. If we behaved ourselves, we are told, cardiovascular disease would decline substantially and the incidence of many cancers would fall. At the same time an increasing array of techniques and drugs are being deployed to arrest the development of these two major remaining killers: statins for all with risky cholesterol levels, angioplasty for blocked arteries and an ever proliferating array of anti-cancer drugs that are now heralded as permitting the management of cancer as a chronic, rather than fatal, condition in the next twenty years.

All of this has succeeded in raising life expectations progressively, so that someone who survives to sixty five can now expect (statistically) to live into their eighties. The prospect hence arises of people dying of nothing except old age and, indeed, funerals are beginning to shift in some cases from bewailing the death and loss of a loved one to the celebration of a long and full life, the Queen Mother's funeral in 2002 being a leading example. Many people still die quite unexpectedly from accidents, disorders and diseases, whether young or old, and it is still an accepted convention to see death as something which intervenes, the grim reaper, over which we exercise no control. It is also often remarked that, with the decline of death as an everyday event among people of all ages, with its dramatic social consequences in orphaned children and young widows and widowers, death has become a taboo. People no longer involve themselves practically in death, which takes place in hospital. Families no longer wash and lay out the body, a service now performed by undertakers. Nor do funerals involve a domestic wake, with mourners paying their respects at an open coffin before the cortège to the funeral at the churchyard. Rather, the deceased is discreetly loaded up on to the hearse and driven to the crematorium for what is, at times, the most perfunctory of ceremonies. Memorial services, which can be held later, with more notice for those travelling from afar, and more fully organised as an appreciation of the life of the deceased, are now finding favour in comparison with traditional burial services.

All of this distracts attention from the process of death itself. That, however, is now increasingly being organised by family and close friends as well as the dying person through a new array of institutions. The inequities in the provision of such care, and the widening discrepancy between what it is possible to provide and what is locally available have recently been addressed by the formation of an all party parliamentary group called Dying Well. Hospitals are now too expensive to be willing to accommodate the terminally ill and/or chronically infirm for extended periods. Those without a hope should be stabilised and given palliative care, either at home or in a hospice, an institution specifically designed for the dying. Those at home should be given specialist domiciliary care, for example from Macmillan nurses in the case of cancer. Those in hospital will be subject to increasingly anxious discussions with relatives as to what interventions to sustain life are acceptable. The letters DNR (for 'do not resuscitate') are written on the records of those who, ideally, have agreed that they do not want violent and invasive procedures such as electro-cardiac stimulation by the crash team, or tracheotomy to open airways. When informed consent is not possible, relatives and medical staff must make the decision as to whether it is in the patient's interest to prolong their life.

Some people have already gone further and written a living will, which specifies that they do not wish to be allowed to exist when dependent upon sustained medical intervention and when incapable of making decisions for themselves.[1] The validity of these wishes as legally significant (they may be countersigned by the doctor) is now accepted. The difficulty arises in respect of their closeness to euthanasia, which is, at the time of writing, still illegal in Britain, although legal in Switzerland, Holland and the state of Oregon in the US. Many remain concerned about those who are severely infirm feeling that they are a burden to family and society, and that they should therefore consent to euthanasia, perhaps against their true wishes. So far only very small numbers have sought the help of specialist organisations abroad to end their lives. Much more widespread is the practice of asking doctors for lethal doses of sedatives, whether directly – 'How many pills do I need doctor?', or 'Please give me a lethal dose of morphine', or indirectly by hoarding drugs and then taking a lethal dose. The grisly career of Harold Shipman, who took advantage of this situation to kill probably several hundred of his patients over an extended period, mostly with morphine injections, most of them elderly, but by no means all seriously infirm, has been a sharp reminder of the dangers of the situation.

One way or another, dying is increasingly extensively organised over longer and longer periods. The greater the advances in medicine in understanding diseases as well as intervening to control and care for those suffering from them, the greater the extent of the advice patients can be offered when conditions cannot be successfully treated. Debate on the prolonging of life hence increasingly focuses on issues around the quality of life that the patient now has and may expect in such a future as may be secured. For those patients who are willing to engage with this discussion, it will be possible for an increasingly precise account to be given for those suffering from a variety of problems. Such sufferers will be able to plan their future in conjunction with services which will need to become accordingly more specialised and extensive and should, if they wish, increasingly be able to plan a death to optimise the quality of life remaining, and to pick a point to die when it promises to decline sharply.

At present far too much of this is ad hoc and full of anxiety. Many of the elderly and dying (by which I do not mean that these two categories necessarily coincide) do not wish to engage with organising their own death. The very success of our society in recent years in keeping death at a distance, and of cultural emphasis upon life, means that there is little legitimate place for the discussion of one's own death. In this respect we should be aware that we differ from a good many societies – ancient Greece and Rome for example, for whom the issue of an honourable and dignified death was a matter of normal public debate and a matter of considerable personal concern. Our culture gives us no experience of such debate, shrouds death with the horror of the unknown and fear of suffering, and provides us with no positive emotional repertoire to discuss our own deaths with equanimity. This will take time to change, but institutions and cultural understandings are evolving quite rapidly already.

Two which will need careful attention in the near future, for reasons of cost as well as their significance for decisions about death, are: the residential care home for the elderly and the nursing home for the elderly. Funding adequate care remains an unresolved issue and inadequate care only accentuates the tendency of these institutions to become warehouses for the dying and invitations to abuse: physical, emotional and financial. Although seen by some, correctly in the better instances, as havens of caring and kindness, these institutions are also viewed by others with alarm and despondency as terminal restraints upon their existence. It might seem a ghoulish joke to envisage a time when children will convene and say: 'Now Dad, it's time to update your death plan. We have got all the latest reviews of your health and prospects, and you need to decide what you want to do in the coming year'. For many, of course, a sudden health crisis will determine the outcome, although again often only to precipitate someone from infirm to moribund and largely incapable, so accentuating the importance of prior expression of wishes. For others, however, such active planning would enhance their sense of as well as the reality of their control over their remaining life and offer, paradoxically, a degree of reassurance.

Those for whom the end of life is most intractable are the mentally disordered, notably through Alzheimer's and other forms of dementia. Here the difficulty is that their mental faculties may decline faster than their physical ones, and decisions about quality of life become very difficult as well as, of course, impossible to discuss with the patient. Earlier expression of wishes, including those on what is to be done or not done in case of mental incapacity are of some benefit, but they can by definition be no complete solution. In this, as, no doubt, in many other cases, death will not be susceptible for many to their own choice and management. For increasing numbers, however, such choices will become more and more possible. The more that they become so, the more people will have the confidence to pursue them, and the more the input of carers and medical staff will become a clear-eyed one of the benefits of various strategies, options and interventions, and the less it will be trammelled by inability to focus on the inevitable and unmentionable. That may make the choices involved more effective and beneficial. It still may not make them easy.

The current debate

So far the campaign for increased public awareness and engagement with the management of dying has been spearheaded by those dying relatively early from degenerative diseases. This has sharply raised the profile of managed death, since the expectation now is that most people will be able to complete their lives. It was because the elderly are expected to be close to death that Harold Shipman was able to continue his murders for so long, since he targeted his elderly patients. The lawsuit by Diane Pretty to clarify the law under the Suicide Act 1961 on the liability of partners and relatives to prosecution for assisting a suicide, which carries a maximum penalty of fourteen years' imprisonment, was rejected by the House of Lords in 2001. She died in 2002. In 2008 Debbie Purdy, also stricken with a degenerative disease, repeated the process, asking the court to require the Director of Public Prosecutions to clarify in what circumstances partners and others would be prosecuted. Once again the court refused, despite hearing evidence that, although there had been no recent prosecutions for assisted suicide, there had been a police investigation in a number of cases, with long delays before decisions were reached.[2]

By this time (2008) the number of Britons travelling to Switzerland to end their lives with the assistance of the organisation Dignitas had passed one hundred. The BMA abandoned its formal opposition to assisted suicide in 2007, adopting a neutral position in which it could campaign neither for nor against it. An attempt by former MP, now Lord, Joel Joffe to introduce a bill on assisted dying for the terminally ill was defeated in the House of Lords, but its sponsor vowed to continue the campaign. In the Scottish Parliament Margo MacDonald, who has Parkinson's disease, announced that she would introduce a Private Member's Bill. The campaign was given further impetus by the trenchant input of Baroness Warnock, who has long advocated the legalisation of euthanasia. She now pointed out the inequity of allowing people to travel abroad to die, since this would only be available to those who could afford to do so. Her views on the right to assisted suicide engaged determinedly with difficult issues:

> During life a person will have been admired if he really
> wanted to do his duty and to do what he regarded as
> in the best interests of his family, his community, or his
> country. He will have been thought well of for not always
> preferring his own interests to those of others. Why then
> when he has reached the end of what he may regard as his

useful life, may he not be allowed to do what he thinks is in the best interests of those he loves, or impersonally in the best interests of the state which is expensively caring for him? Why may not someone who has always really wanted to behave well be recognised and admired in continuing that desire in asking for death?[3]

The standard concerns here are fears that others may put pressure on the infirm to opt for suicide, whether or not the pressure is intentional; the difficulty of being sure that death is indeed what the person wants – suicide attempts notoriously contain a significant proportion of 'cries for help'; and the rights and interests of relatives, who may suffer by being so formally abandoned. The most problematic issue, however, is ensuring that the would-be suicide is mentally competent, especially where dementia is involved, and the great difficulty in acting on clear wishes expressed earlier in a 'living will'. The paradox is that the one thing many people fear most is being trapped in a failing mind that robs them of the capacity to act, but not to suffer; yet, even if they express a wish to die in such circumstances clearly in writing, their relatives may find it very hard to follow those wishes some years later, since they cannot be sure that, when faced with the reality, the writer of the will would still wish to die. Warnock's views are firm:

> With seven hundred thousand people suffering [Alzheimer's] it really is a problem that has to be faced. The fact is we have to take a fairly unsentimental view. Care may get better, but if so at large cost. There is no point in saying we ought to spend more, because we can't. People talk about it as if the only respectable motive for wanting to die is your own sake. But it seems to me just as respectable to want to die partly for the sake of others and for the sake of society.[4]

A slightly different take on the issues was offered by Guy Brown, a research biochemist who switched from investigating cancer to Alzheimer's as he recognised the severity of the issues involved. He pointed out that our lives have been greatly extended in the past generation or two, but that the quality of life available in the additional years is very variable: for some it is good, for others poor and getting worse, culminating in great suffering. Alzheimer's in particular is an unpleasant degenerative disease, yet funding for research on it is only three per cent of that directed at cancer: 'We are going to reach some kind of tipping point at the middle of this century when fifty per cent of people are going to die with dementia'.[5]

The problems of care

If managing our death is the new and, for many, extremely intractable issue, these points about infirmity, loss of capacity and quality of life point to another difficult set of choices for many. How do we manage our lives when we are progressively less able to care for ourselves? The options here are well-established and work well for some, but are often fraught. How much practical care should be expected from children and other relatives? What right have we to demand a substantial input that may go on for twenty years, taking them into old age themselves? Can we afford private care, and to what extent should the state provide? In Scotland it does, whereas in England medical care is free but social care is means tested, often meaning that the person's home has to be sold to fund long-term care. How adequate and reliable will sheltered accommodation or residential care be? The elderly and infirm are least well-equipped to defend their interests and, in the absence of relatives to support them, they can become warehoused or abused. Nor is the quality of an establishment to be relied upon: staff change, ownership changes, there are constant pressures on finances and, although there are major players in the care market, establishments go out of business constantly because of cost pressures. None of this is made easier by the constant rearranging of the regulatory framework, with standards being revised and inspection authorities reorganised.[6] To be sure, all of this is being done with the object of securing and enhancing standards of care and, at least in part, in response to persistent evidence of serious abuses, but it is very far from achieving a secure and predictable environment for those seeking care for themselves or their relatives.

Care of the elderly has always been problematic. The belief that they were cherished by and dispensed wisdom to their extended families in the past is probably only as much half true as the claim that they were neglected, abused and derided. Both, after all, happen today, but today they happen to far more people for far longer, and in a society in which expectations of rights to a civilised and bearable existence for all have become entrenched. Achieving that for the elderly and infirm is a challenge that has not been met, and for the families who are faced with it, whether as elderly individuals or couples, or their relatives, it is singularly intractable.

Part Three

Conclusions

TWELVE

Choice and meaning

Choice requires context if it is to be meaningful and intelligible. Children sometimes ask adults questions such as: what is your favourite colour? Your favourite number? No doubt most of us would recognise vague sentiments in respect of these questions but, unless we have a specific context, for example an interest in mathematics or gambling, or a strong concern with interior design, it is difficult for us to mobilise an answer. The main reason for this is because we cannot identify clear reasons that we would accept as compelling for one preference or another. What sustains this context? A reasonably stable culture in a reasonably stable society.

Our society is paradoxical in this respect. On the one hand it has the stability of success. It is not seriously threatened by external aggression or internal faction. Its trade, culture and language have been successfully exported globally. It has immensely powerful allies – political, cultural and economic. Yet, as we have seen, change is part of this success, and the emphasis on change as a condition of continued participation in success, primarily economic but derivatively in most other respects, has become ever more insistent. Keeping up with those changes and, by the sum of our choices, driving the changes, requires constant adaptation, fresh choices. We attempt to construct stability for ourselves, a stable personal way of life, with routines, habits, secure income, stable relationships and work, within the overall context of our sense of our future and what we hope for in that future. In this we are no different from our ancestors.

What we lack are secure guidelines reassuring us that we have got it right. We throw out sea anchors to at least slow down our movement on the ocean of possibilities: we try to identify work which will be fulfilling as well as financially rewarding and tolerably secure, and so acquire elements of a personal social identity and a set of reference points; we attempt to establish primary relationships to provide ourselves with someone who understands and is committed to us regardless of events and over the long term; we have children, whose care and prospects provide an intense and rewarding focus; we maintain networks of friends and family, whose emotional significance and participation in our lives over the long term give perspective and stability. Yet in each of these instances many of us do not succeed in maintaining much stability. Not only is work hard to sustain, we are explicitly required to be flexible in today's economy and society in order to succeed. Our primary relationships frequently fail and cause more confusion and crisis than security and stability; our children are often the victims of this, and we can, in any case, offer them little sensible advice and security once they move beyond school. Many people find it hard to maintain friends and contacts with family during lives that take them over great distances into changing social and economic circumstances, and in which they find immediate sustenance in new friends and acquaintances, which they can shed as these relationships become redundant, in an ever evolving network.

Not only are work and family no longer reliable, although still essential to most in grounding us, but an increasingly large area lies beyond their capacity to engage and advise effectively. The success of the social democratic project and incessantly increasing affluence has already reduced for most of us the grinding necessity of the struggle for survival. At the same time the radical individualism which has been insisted upon in the consumer society has reduced the social ties that rooted us in the past in community, class, religion, region and ethnicity. We do not need to be tied to all that stuff any more; we are citizens of the world, free to do as we choose, and to choose when, where and how long we do it. This allows us a vast and constantly evolving range of lifestyle choices: where, when, how long and how far to travel, which sports and hobbies to pursue and, then, if they really become absorbing, whether to convert them into work (skier to ski instructor), what kind of home to live in and how to furnish it, what kind of food to eat and which drugs to enjoy, what kind of body to cultivate, what kind of personal appearance and style to maintain, which form of religion, spiritual healing, therapy or personal development to pursue. This glittering kaleidoscope, ever twisting, enjoins us to choose ourselves, to decide who we are and

what we want to be; until that is, the still, small voice inside us asks:
but what is the point?

Religion as a support for meaning

For those with the leisure and the inclination to stop to think about
such questions in the past the answer was apparently provided by
religion. I say 'apparently', meaning that is the way it appeared.
Religion did and does address issues of fundamental meaning, but
religion was established in society. Even where it was not an official
religion, most societies have had one dominant religion which
informed and sustained, and in turn was informed and sustained by,
the status quo. In a crude sense this had to mean that religion was
supportive of the prevailing political order, whether of the Pharaohs,
of the medieval European monarchs, or of the Ottoman Empire.
More widely and substantially, however, a dominant religion engaged
with every aspect of society – its family life, its cultural output in
painting, plays and science, its trading practices, its leisure pursuits –
and provided guidance. Religion and culture were hence inevitable
reflections of each other and mutually sustaining. Religion today
has become also a matter of choice, and cannot function in this way.
Church of England? Which bit? It is likely shortly to split in two
over the issue of homosexuality. Besides, some members believe
in God in a traditional sense and in most of the New Testament,
whereas others believe in little more than a benign force and in
the Bible as a useful source of moral inspiration if treated critically.
Fancy a bit of Kabbalah? It used to be a part of Judaism, but is
now run independently for the spiritual enlightenment of some,
celebrities among them. Is Scientology a religion? It claims it is, and
is more successful in its size and revenue earning than many kinds
of Christianity. Religion works as a social institution which secures
the meaningfulness of people's existence in societies when it is just
there, taken for granted, inevitable. When not only can you opt out,
but when religion is yet another consumer choice, its role is reversed
and humiliated. If religion is to have any authority it must be capable
of active guidance of people's lives by deriving influence from every
quarter. It is not a question of 'what works for you'.

The other form in which religion succeeds in sustaining meaning for believers is sectarianism. Here the faithful are constantly aware of their minority situation in a world of the benighted, but this only reinforces their faith and they sustain one another. Sectarianism may take an interned route and believers cut themselves off from the rest of society, at the extreme in highly segregated cults, or may turn outwards to evangelism. In either case security derives from emphasising the polarity between believers who have seen the light and are saved and the unhappy infidels who have not. Such sectarianism can also take an overtly political form, which is just as effective as long as it can be sustained in giving meaning to the existence of adherents: the revolutionary party, whether nationalist or socialist, the dedicated campaign group, whether for animal rights or environmental causes. The difficulty for the sectarian strategy in the liberal, sceptical, rationalistic and tolerant society in which we live is that its moral and intellectual closure and tendency to fanaticism restricts its appeal. For many it smacks of desperation and its intellectual rigidity is incapable of engaging with the detached critic who says: 'I agree you have a point, but ...'. There are no 'buts' for sectarians, for 'buts' lead to the questioning of principles and articles of faith.

There is of course a religious faction that believes in the re-establishment of religion in a dominant form, the Taliban who ruled Afghanistan and gave refuge and support to Osama bin Laden. The decadence, as they would see it, of Western society, indulging in gross and hedonistic individualised choice is partly what has inspired Islamic fundamentalists to a radical defence, a regime which industrialised democracies see as religious totalitarianism. Emile Durkheim, writing on industrialisation and its consequences a century ago, was also concerned about the impact, not just of the decline of organised religion, but of the rise of individualism.[1] His term for the slide into meaninglessness was 'anomie': the collapse in the meaning of rules. Tolerance, he observed, had become a driving necessity of industrialised democracy and eventually put everything up for question, insisted on fewer and fewer commitments in terms of rules and values, and led to relativistic morality and culture.

Developments since then have only enhanced the sources of his concern.

Individualism and the retreat into self in the search for meaning: hedonism

What is our reaction to the need to struggle to sustain meaning in a world in which secure conclusions are constantly undermined by the offer of alternatives? It is, in an individualistic world, to do what we know how to do: to retreat ever further into ourselves. We do not do this most of the time (at least most of us do not). Much of the time the demands of running a practical life and earning a living dominate, as they always have. Much of our spare time is spent on what might now be called ruthless hedonism: pushing the limits of indulgence, most publicly in binge drinking and drug taking, but just as much in obsessional refinement of food and cuisine, exotic recreations with powerful sensations such as paragliding and surfing, which have their mass market counterparts in theme parks, in searching for the perfect holiday retreat, in films and music presented in ever more flamboyant and sensually overwhelming ways, in the idealisation of sporting heroes and events, now cast as a way of life for fans. Such recreations fill the gap while they last. Their answer to the question 'What is the point?' is: 'You don't really need there to be a point in a cosmic sense. The point is it feels good and I feel good. That's enough.'

Such sentiments have been skilfully elaborated by those, on the one hand, who would be embarrassed at over-reliance on what used to be called 'cheap thrills', and, on the other, by those only too willing to provide specialised experiences for the affluent. With the satisfaction from purchases of ever more material goods beginning to reach saturation point for the affluent, what has come to be called the 'experience economy' has developed. Skiing has long had a place in the pantheon of experience. At one level it is pure sensation, exhilarating and exciting, but at the same time it is also a sport which requires great skill if one is to excel. It has also historically been expensive to pursue and hence socially exclusive. Cheap travel and mass tourism have dramatically reduced costs and the introduction of the snowboard has made getting started more socially accessible, especially for a generation reared on skateboards. Insofar as experience means more than sensation, and hence goes beyond hedonism and the adrenalin rush to involve the acquisition of skill and knowledge, it can lay claim to making a more plausible contribution to self-development and self-fulfilment, and hence to plugging the meaning gap.

Such pursuits are, however, vulnerable to status degradation. When the ski resort is crammed full of novice skiers clattering into one another on the piste, who are as much focused on riotous and debauched après-ski as on honing their downhill skills, somehow the attraction is lessened. Tourist destinations more widely have for some time been subject to the same process of degradation: what begins as a magical discovery known to the few becomes, in time, the must visit place for the cognoscenti, and ends up as a package tour destination indistinguishable from scores of others and dominated by internationalised hotels and restaurants. The 'experience' option widens tourism to include food, sports, 'adventure' and experiences such as paintballing, white-water rafting and ecotourism.

The retreat into self: self-improvement

Self-improvement is a further step down the same road. Meaning is created by longer-term and more substantial engagement, whether this is a specific skill like watercolour painting or learning a language, or a route to self-knowledge like yoga or meditation, or delving into the arts, culture and history. Here there is more disciplined and more extensive knowledge, and more feedback from the accumulated human knowledge with which one must engage. It is far from buying sensation and it engages more with the sources of meaning by learning to understand how human societies and individuals have created meaning over time and space.

Those who do persist and ask questions are driven back upon themselves and find no self-evident answer. Many struggle, a few are inspired with a specific solution and others construct a more or less satisfactory one by their own lights. All are vulnerable to being overtaken by developments, however. Even so fundamental and traditional a desire as wanting to see the benefits of industrialisation in respect of adequate food, shelter and services spread throughout the world is compromised: fifty years of aid to Africa, the poorest continent, have produced war, plague, corruption, poverty, drought and famine. Africa needs help, but evidently not of the kind it has received.

Choice and meaning: three options

If meaning and direction is subject to choice, there are really only three options. The first is to continue the rationalist grind and to accept that the price of this is lack of closure. There are no ultimate answers, and that is the consequence of the path upon which we have embarked. Such answers that we as individuals and groups come up with are revealed regularly as conditional, as the assumptions we had not thought about or known about become evident, and then questioned. We know that those in the past who thought they lived in a secure world of meaning, where the rising of the sun and the rotation of the seasons were secured by the propitiation of the gods, were mistaken. If we relinquish the superstition and revealed truth of religion we have only the conjectures and refutations of science to rely upon. We now know that we do not have ultimate security, only relative. For some, that limited knowledge and escape from the comforting fantasies of the past is a better source of security, even though, like platforms built to live on a marsh, the theories of science need constant maintenance in use and complete rebuilding from time to time.[2] Marshes are very fertile, diverse and interesting places; they are dangerous and you can be engulfed, but people live in them quite successfully.

The second option is conversion to some form of certainty buttressed by powerful beliefs. For some this is still a religion. For others it may be a political doctrine, these days more often issue based than comprehensive. For far too many it is finding the one other person who will complement and sustain them, understand and care for them, and with whom there will be perfect, perpetual, mutual devotion. As we have seen earlier, love, in this modern romantic form, is rarely able to bear this burden of expectation, although, like work and family, it can make a contribution. The significant feature of all the varieties of practical recourse in this option is that the conversion process, falling in love, is projected to appear as though it comes from without and takes charge although in reality it comes from within the individual. This produces decisions which seem inevitable and overwhelmingly right and good. End of problem. Others, of course, see your 'conversion' as manifest delusion. From your point of view that is their loss.

The final option is one which is becoming ever more popular: the retreat into personal feelings. It is almost as though a generation had lit upon a development of Descartes which elegantly reverses everything that he and the subsequent progress of rationality has stood for: 'I think therefore I am' has become 'I feel therefore I know'. Both the difficulty and the satisfaction derive from being certain what you feel, and hence what you know. The great advantage of this strategy is that it 'needs no equipment or special training'. Our feelings are uniquely accessible to ourselves and, for some, may constitute a substantial part of the experience of selfhood. Other people can discuss our feelings and sometimes help us pinpoint what they are, but they are wholly reliant on us for evidence of what *we feel*. Further, feelings are at times, and for many at most times, self-validating and self-explanatory. Hence, whilst we can discuss, for example, why we could never vote Tory, why we hate football, why a particular performance of Beethoven's Eroica was sublimely uplifting, why sleeping with your partner's sister or brother is an important exploration and personal development or, as the case may be, why it is wrong, why animal experiments are right or wrong, and whether free speech is indivisible, those who go down the feeling route preclude further debate at a certain point with the assertion: 'That's just the way I feel about it'. The reply: 'So who gives a damn; the question is: are you right?', elicits a rather odd look and the eventual riposte: 'That's my opinion (and it's as good as any, yours included)'. This style of managing reality is displayed in the substitution of 'feel' in giving opinions: 'I feel' instead of 'I think', or 'I believe'; and in discussions which are directed at eliciting sentiment on the topic under discussion rather than reasoned debate: how do we all feel about this proposal?

It is important to recognise that this is the opposite of the genuine exploration of feelings that was initiated by Freud and his generation, and which has given rise to varieties of therapy. Here, although the initial question may be to uncover what feelings are lurking unacknowledged, the explanatory one is to find out where they came from, and the therapy consists, in most cases, in recognising that they are an inappropriate, disproportionate or historically redundant response, which can be safely abandoned. This process is one of exploring feelings with the object of subjecting them to rational investigation and analysis. This is based on the assumption that feelings are responses to situations which may or may not be justifiable, rather than seeing them as being self-justificatory by definition. The attraction of feelings for those who have recourse to them as the solution to the unending dilemmas of choice is that they seem to offer closure. That is what you feel, ergo that is what you must now do, because you want to, and it is right to do so. For the genuine believer in feelings the fact that they may change is no obstacle, since they are just as self-validating. The awkward cuss who asks why you believe one thing to be correct now, when you believed another earlier, may receive an answer in terms of the information or experiences that led to the change of feelings, but the point is that you cannot legitimately intervene and question the views or interpretations. That is how it was, and that is what I now hold, and to challenge it is to fail to respect my feelings. This kind of emotional solipsism may be pitiful to behold, but it is powerful enough as a collectively held position to command indignation if it is challenged. 'Upsetting' people without very good cause is now quite established as wicked. If you disagree, stay shtum, even if you believe it is in the other person's own interest to question their views and feelings. Look for others with whom you can share your views without upset. This is one of the further advances of tolerance: everyone must be permitted to cleave to whatever they believe because of what they feel.

THIRTEEN

Conclusion

This book has attempted to unpick the taken for granted character of choice in our society, to explore what it is and identify where it came from. There is no question of our going back to the traditional form of society in which choices were much more limited and structured. Our society has been characterised, especially with the impact of industrialisation over the past two centuries, by a very rapid rate of change in almost all areas of life; changes which have introduced new choices and continue to do so. Yet, as we saw in Part One, choice is Janus faced. Its introduction allows people more control of their lives, at least in a nominal sense. Whether it gives real control depends upon whether they have understood the options facing them, and whether those options are being managed by others to appear in particular ways. At the same time, too many choices overwhelm and oppress us. Everyone has their comfort level and most of us have learned to raise this to take advantage of what is available. In terms of the balance between choice as empowering and overwhelming there is hence an optimum for each individual and collectively for each society. This, I suggest, is something that a society such as ours would do well to reflect upon, rather than blindly accepting that choice and more choice is always for the better. Rather than a necessary benefit, choice at some level is a limitation, and a society that aims to progress and improve itself should know its limitations. Chapters Four and Five illustrated a variety of circumstances in which choice does not work well as an institutional mechanism, and identified provision as an at times more effective one.

Choice is also individualising, particularly in our market-based society and economy. Of course choices can be collective, but the overwhelming majority of those we make are effectively individual. More to the point, we see ourselves and are seen by others as responsible for our choices. In many respects they are the basis of how we advance and achieve, or how we fail to do so. This increases the pressure on us. If we succeed, we feel bullish – the achievement is ours as individuals; if we do not, the failure is also down to us. Yet there are so many choices, many of them of such complexity (and sometimes of a complexity which we do not necessarily appreciate at the time), that most of us are very unlikely to make good choices all of the time.

Part Two has contrasted market-based choices with those that now arise for all of us across our lives. These, as we have seen, are much bigger and often intractable choices. One might hope that we would have therefore worked out ways to ensure that most people succeeded in them; either that, or allowed ways of opting out. Neither is the case. Like the market-based choices, the momentous ones of the life cycle are down to us as individuals. Unlike them, there is almost nothing in our social and cultural repertoire available by way of provision as an alternative to individual choice. Yet getting them right, from entry into the job market to our eventual demise, can regularly make the difference between a legitimate sense of fulfilment and personal misery. Support and advice can be provided by intermediaries to assist in these choices, but it is just that, advice. The choice is down to us and this is as it should be, since these important choices are mostly ones that have been earned, in some cases struggled for cumulatively for centuries as individual rights. Now we have them, making the decisions is not easy; getting them wrong or ineffective often has dire negative consequences and attempting to opt out by refusing to make the choice may well make things worse. In each case we may well regard it as unthinkable to return to the past and in each case we may regard the travails involved as worthwhile; collectively, however, the downside is considerable.

For the more resolute of us – and we have certainly been taught as a society to be resolute about choice – all this is simply the price that has to be paid for the advantages of choice. We would not want to go back to a society that did not have them, or only in a very attenuated form. But we have greater expectations than that: that the extensive, at least apparent, control of our lives that widespread choice confers will enable us to live the life we want and to be the people we want to be, which will make us fulfilled and happy: why else bear the burden of constant choices at different levels of consequence and complexity? A society in which people can make more choices, are less disenfranchised, constrained and disadvantaged is, unsurprisingly, a society in which the pursuit of happiness is an important goal. There is, of course, a view that happiness only comes to those who do not pursue it, and that to do so is to pursue a mirage. That apart, the world of constant choice, from the trivial to the momentous, has emerged as a world of great uncertainty, with great pressure on the individual and, in respect of at least some major choices for many, as much a source of anguish as fulfilment. It may be argued that this is nonetheless a worthwhile place to be; it is harder to maintain that it is a happy place to be. Choice, then, is more a Pandora's box than a panacea, though this analogy should not be pushed too far; at the bottom of Pandora's box, a myth from ancient Greece, lay hope. At the bottom of choice lies expectation. The outcome of the repeated calculations of choice is satisfaction at success and frustration at the lack of it. The shift of responsibility from fate to chooser, however, elicits a sustained anxiety about successful choice.

Notes and sources

Preface

[1] Schwartz, B. (2004) *The paradox of choice: Why more is less*, New York, NY: Ecco/Harper Collins.

Chapter One

[1] Leeson's account of his exploits can be found in:
> Leeson, N.W. and Whitley, E. (1996) *Rogue trader: How I brought down Barings and shook the financial world*, New York, NY: Little, Brown.

See also:
> Rawnsley, J.H. (1995) *Going for broke: Nick Leeson and the collapse of Barings Bank*, New York, NY: Harper Collins.

[2] Schwartz, B. (2004) *The paradox of choice: Why more is less*, New York, NY: Ecco/Harper Collins, p 114.

[3] Berger, P. and Luckmann, T. (1967) *The social construction of reality*, London: Allen Lane.

Chapter Two

[1] Much of this chapter draws on Schwartz, B. (2004) *The paradox of choice: Why more is less*, New York, NY: Ecco/Harper Collins.

[2] For Herbert Simon's analysis see:
> Simon, H. (1956) 'Rational choice and the structure of the environment', *Psychological Review*, vol 63, pp 129–38.
> Simon, H. (1957) *Models of man, social and rational*, New York, NY: John Wiley.

[3] Wyse, D., McCreery, E. and Torrance, H. (2008) *The trajectory and impact of national reform: Curriculum and assessment in English primary schools*, Cambridge: Cambridge University Faculty of Education.

[4] Lukes, S.T. (1973) *Individualism*, Oxford: Blackwell.

[5] Schwartz, B. (2004) *The paradox of choice: Why more is less*, New York, NY: Ecco/Harper Collins, ch 8.

[6] Hirsch, F. (1977) *Social limits to growth*, London: Routledge & Kegan Paul.

Chapter Three

[1] For a more extended account of the consumer society see, for example:

Bauman, Z. (2007) *Consuming life*, Cambridge: Polity.

Paterson, M. (2005) *Consumption and everyday life*, London: Routledge.

Gabriel, Y. and Lang, T. (1995) *The unmanageable consumer*, London: Routledge.

Benson, J. (1994) *The rise of consumer society in Britain 1880–1980*, London: Longman.

Giddens, A. (1991) *Modernity and self identity*, Cambridge, Polity.

[2] See:

Lukes, S.T. (1973) *Individualism*, Oxford: Blackwell.

Nisbet, R.A. (1980) *History of the idea of progress*, New York, NY: Basic Books.

Sklair, L. (1998) *The sociology of progress*, London: Routledge.

[3] For a history of industrialisation see:

Hobsbawm, E. (1969) *Industry and empire: An economic history of Britain since 1750*, London: Penguin.

[4] See, for example:

Musson, A.E. and Robinson, E. (1969) *Science and technology in the Industrial Revolution*, Manchester: Manchester University Press.

[5] See the work of:

Hill, C. (1965) *Intellectual origins of the English revolution, 1530–1780*, Oxford: Oxford University Press.

Nenner, H. (1977) *By colour of law: Legal culture and constitutional politics in England*, Chicago, IL: Chicago University Press.

[6] See E.P. Thompson's comments in (1968) *The making of the English working class*, Harmondsworth: Penguin.

[7] Nisbet, N.A. (1980) *History of the idea of progress*, New York, NY: Basic Books.

[8] For example, four English monarchs were deposed in the fourteenth and fifteenth centuries.

[9] Baumol, W.J., Landes, D.S. and Mokyr, J. (eds) (2008) *Entrepreneurs and entrepreneurship in economic history*, Princeton, NJ: Princeton University Press.

[10] Atiyah, P.S. (1979) *The rise and fall of freedom of contract*, Oxford: Oxford University Press.

[11] Keynes, J.M. (1923) *A tract on monetary reform*, London: Macmillan.

[12] See:

> Keith, M. (1993) *Race riots and policing: Lore and disorder in a multi-racist society*, London: UCL Press.
>
> Waddington, D. (1992) *Contemporary issues in public disorder: A comparative and historical approach*, London: Routledge.

[13] See:

> Bruce, M. (1961) *The coming of the welfare state*, London: Routledge.
>
> Mommsen, W.J. and Mock, W. (1981) *Welfare states in Britain and Germany*, London: German Historical Institute.
>
> Mau, S. (2003) *The moral economy of welfare states: Britain and Germany compared*, London: Routledge.

[14] Hennessy, P. (1992) *Never again: Britain 1945–51*, London: Jonathan Cape.

[15] See:

> Goldthorpe, J.H., Lockwood, D. et al (1969) *The affluent worker in the class structure*, Cambridge: Cambridge University Press.
>
> Goldthorpe, J.H. (1980) *Social mobility and class structure in modern Britain*, Oxford: Clarendon Press.

[16] In his speech to the Conservative rally, Bedford, 20 May 1957.

[17] Galbraith, J.K. (1999) *The affluent society*, new edn, London: Penguin.

[18] See:

> Goldthorpe, J.H., Lockwood, D. et al (1969) *The affluent worker in the class structure*, Cambridge: Cambridge University Press.
>
> Goldthorpe, J.H., Lockwood, D. et al (1968) *The affluent worker: Industrial attitudes and behaviour*, Cambridge: Cambridge University Press.

Goldthorpe, J.H., Lockwood, D. et al (1968) *The affluent worker: Political attitudes and behaviour*, Cambridge: Cambridge University Press.

[19] Conversation with *Woman's Own* magazine, 31 October 1987.

[20] Mills, C.W. (1951) *White collar: The American middle classes*, Oxford: Oxford University Press.

See also:

Sennett, R. (1978) *The fall of public man: On the social psychology of capitalism*, New York, NY: Vintage.

[21] Clarke, M.J. (1999) *Citizens' financial futures: The regulation of retail financial services in Britain*, Aldershot: Ashgate.

[22] Durkheim, E. (1964) *The division of labour*, New York, NY: The Free Press.

See also:

Lukes, S. (1972) *Emile Durkheim: His life and work*, New York, NY: Harper and Row.

Chapter Four

[1] There is a substantial literature on the professions. A good brief overview of some of the issues they raise is to be found in:

Johnson, T. (1967) *Professions and power*, Basingstoke: Macmillan.

A different and more complex account is available in:

Abbot, A. (1988) *The system of professions*, Chicago, IL: University of Chicago Press.

[2] The unreliability of even the most established of professions is amply demonstrated by solicitors. The 140,000 members of the Law Society were the subject of 20,902 complaints in 2008–09, up 7% on the previous year and the latest in a tide that had been flooding for many years. Frustration at the handling of complaints by the Law Society, and particularly its delays in processing them, had been mounting for years and was eventually recognised by government which, in the Access to Justice Act 1999, provided for the appointment of an independent commissioner if practice did not improve. The Law Society's competence to investigate complaints against its members was subject to increasing pressure, and a greater measure of independence was progressively established

in the complaints handling body, which was repeatedly reconfigured. Despite further warnings matters did not improve significantly and a Legal Complaints Commissioner was appointed in 2004, overseeing a now independent Legal Complaints Service. Some improvement took place, but penalties were imposed for inadequate performance in 2008 and 2009. The system will be restructured again in 2010 under the Office for Legal Complaints and the Legal Services Board, which will have oversight of all branches of the legal profession. Complaints may eventually get responded to in a timely, fair and competent way; whether their numbers will decline is another matter.

See The Legal Services Complaints Commissioner's Annual Report and Accounts 2008–2009, *Opportunity for Excellence*, HC 651, London: The Stationery Office, 2009, www.olscc.gov.uk/publications

[3] A sceptical view of self-help books written by a former insider is provided in Salerno, S. (2005) *Sham: How the gurus of the self-help movement make us helpless*, London: Nicholas Brealey Publishing.

[4] The history and services of the National Missing Persons Helpline can be found at www.missingpeople.org.uk

[5] See www.chooseandbook.nhs.uk

[6] Audit Commission (2005) *Early lessons on payment by results*, London: Audit Commission.

[7] Department of Health (2008) *High quality health care for all*, Cm 7432 (The Darzi Report), London: Department of Health.

[8] Clarke, M.J. (1999) *Citizens' financial futures: The regulation of retail financial services*, Aldershot: Ashgate.

[9] The Equitable Life debacle has been exhaustively investigated in two official reports:

Penrose, Lord (2004) *Report on the Equitable Life Inquiry*, HC 290, London: The Stationery Office.

Abraham, A. (Parliamentary Commissioner for Administration) (2008) *Equitable Life: A catalogue of regulatory failure*, HC Paper 815, Session 2007–08.

[10] Anderson, C. (2006) *The long tail: How endless choice is creating unlimited demand*, New York, NY: Random House.

[11] The history of pop music has been widely discussed. For an entertaining review of it up to its heyday see:

Cohn, N. (1970) *Awopbopaloopbop Alopbamboom: Pop from the beginning*, London: Paladin.

For accounts and analysis up to more recent times see:

Longhurst, B. (2007) *Popular music and society*, Cambridge: Polity.

Frith, S., Straw, W. and Street, J. (eds) (2001) *Cambridge companion to pop and rock*, Cambridge: Cambridge University Press.

Frith, S. (1996) *Performing rites: On the value of popular music*, Cambridge, MA: Harvard University Press.

[12] Sir David Attenborough and Stephen Fry gave their lectures on 30 April and 5 May 2008, and they were broadcast on BBC Parliament. The lectures were subsequently available at www.bbc.co.uk/thefuture

[13] In a Defense Department news conference, 12 February 2002.

Chapter Five

[1] The concentration of industries into ever larger and fewer firms was a principal mechanism identified by Marx which would propel capitalism into crisis, as increasing masses of employees were confronted by fewer, but ever richer, employers. A classic account of this process, though without of course quite the outcome Marx anticipated, is provided by:

Baran, P.A. and Sweezy, P.M. (1966) *Monopoly capital: An essay on the American economic and social order*, New York, NY: Monthly Review Press.

For more recent accounts by an economist see:

Utton, M.A. (1986) *Profits and the stability of monopoly*, Cambridge: Cambridge University Press.

Utton, M.A. (2003) *Market domination and anti-trust policy*, Aldershot: Edward Elgar.

[2] The work, including reports of investigations into particular cases, by the Office of Fair Trading, the Competition Commission and the European Union Competition Commissioner is available from their websites:

www.oft.gov.uk

www.competition-commission.org.uk

www.mmc.gov.uk

www.ec.europa.eu/competion

[3] House of Commons Business and Enterprise Select Committee (2009) *Pub Companies, Seventh Report of Session 2008–09*, HC-26i, London: The Stationery Office.

[4] Ibid, p 4.

[5] The American consumer rights campaigner and latterly presidential candidate Ralph Nader scored an early hit with his 1965 *Unsafe at any speed*, New York, NY: Grossman.

[6] On leaded petrol see the work of another doughty campaigner:

Wilson, D. (1983) *The lead scandal*, London: Heinemann.

[7] Matters move so fast that reporting in the professional and financial press and reactions by the regulators are the only way to keep up, though the Consumers' Association, now known as Which?, has also played a useful role. See its website – www.which.co.uk – and that of the Financial Services Authority – www.fsa.gov.uk

[8] By way of example, action by the Financial Services Authority for the mis-selling of payment protection insurance involved nineteen firms between September 2006 and December 2008. The larger fines imposed included Alliance and Leicester £7,000,000, HFC Bank £1,085,000, Liverpool Victoria Banking £840,000, Egg £721,000, GE Capital Bank £610,000, Loans.co.uk £4,550,000, Land of Leather £210,000.

For a review of how things developed at an earlier stage see:

Clarke, M.J. (1998) *Citizens' financial futures*, Aldershot, Ashgate.

[9] Robert McNamara made his remark about the Cuban missile crisis in the film directed by Errol Morris, *Fog of War*, released by Columbia Pictures in 2003.

[10] For a good account of the stock market bubble which preceded the credit crunch and market crash of 2008 see:

Cassidy, J. (2002) *dot.con*, London: Allen Lane.

Chapter Six

[1] Goldthorpe, J.H. (1980) *Social mobility and class structure in modern Britain*, Oxford: Oxford University Press.

[2] Laslett, P. (1991) *A fresh map of life: The emergence of the Third Age*, Cambridge, MA: Harvard University Press.

[3] Giddens, A. (1991) *Modernity and self-identity*, Cambridge: Polity; see also Chapter Two.

[4] This constant comparison is exacerbated, as Schwartz states:

> When we engage in our inevitable social comparisons, to whom do we compare ourselves? In earlier times, such comparisons were necessarily local. We looked around our neighbours and family members. We didn't have access to information about people outside our immediate social circle. But with the explosion of telecommunications – TVs, movies, the internet – almost everyone has access to information about everyone else. (Schwartz, B. (2004) *The paradox of choice: Why more is less*, New York, NY: Ecco/Harper Collins, pp 190–1)

Chapter Seven

[1] There is a vast literature on the nature of work, but much of it explores matters from the vantage point of management, and, even if not, usually from a vantage point inside the organisation. One particularly insightful researcher who writes from the vantage point of the person working through life is Richard Sennett. See:

Sennett, R. (1978) *The fall of public man: On the social psychology of capitalism*, New York, NY: Vintage.

Sennett, R. (1998) *The corrosion of character: The personal consequences of the new capitalism*, New York, NY: W.W. Norton.

Sennett, R. (2004) *Respect in a world of inequality*, New York, NY: W.W. Norton.

[2] The 'angry young men' were Kingsley Amis, John Braine, John Osbourne, John Wain, Kenneth Tynan and Lindsay Anderson. See Ratcliffe, M. (2009) 'Angry young men', *Dictionary of National Biography*, online edition, Oxford: Oxford University Press, at www.oxforddnb/view/theme/95563/

[3] Whyte, W.H. (1963) *The organisation man*, London: Penguin.

Chapter Eight

[1] For an account of the history of romantic love see:

> de Rougement, D. (1956) *Love in the western world*, New York, NY: Pantheon.

Further thoughts on love and love-based relationships are to be found in:

> Giddens, A. (1991) *Modernity and self-identity*, Cambridge: Polity.

See also:

> Goode, W.J. (1959) 'The theoretical importance of love', *American Sociological Review*, vol 24, pp 38-47.

[2] Research on 'living apart together' is available in *Population Trends* 122, Winter 2005, at www.statistics.gov.uk/statbase/product. asp?vink=6303

Chapter Nine

[1] See: Inquiry into the management of care of children receiving complex heart surgery at the Bristol Royal Infirmary, Final Report, July 2001, Cm 5207, HMSO.

[2] At least some members of nearly all societies have endeavoured to control their fertility, with widely varying degrees of moral hesitation (as with some Catholics today) and energy. Their efforts did not become reliable and widely accessible until the introduction of the contraceptive pill and wide distribution of advice on barrier methods in the 1960s. For an account of England in earlier times see the work of:

> Laslett, P. (1973) *The world we have lost: England before the Industrial Age*, Upper Saddle River, NJ: Prentice Hall; rev edn, 1983, Cambridge: Cambridge University Press.

> Laslett, P. (1977) *Family life and illicit love in earlier generations*, Cambridge: Cambridge University Press.

> Laslett, P. and Wall, R. (eds) (1987) *Household and family in past times*, Cambridge: Cambridge University Press.

Even in the early twentieth century Marie Stopes was motivated to campaign for the distribution of contraceptive advice and equipment by her experience of the ignorance of most of the (married) female population, although she wrote explicitly for the middle and upper classes. She was confronted with outrage from some quarters at the immorality of such an unnatural practice. See her *Married life*, originally published in 1918, reprinted by Oxford University Press in 2004.

[3] We are now not only able to delay fertility until we are ready, but to conjure it up as late as we wish (although as pointed out, not with any certainty). The oldest mothers now give birth beyond 65. See, for example:

> Catan, T. (2007) 'Woman who lied to get IVF at 67 seeks a younger husband to help with twins', *The Times*, 27 January.

[4] The IPPR research referred to is available in:

> Dixon, M. and Margo, J. (2006) 'Population politics', 22 February, at www.ippr.org.uk/articles

[5] Information on the prediction of fertility by egg numbers is available from the American Society for Reproductive Medicine, Patients' fact sheet: 'Prediction of fertility potential from ovarian reserves in women', at www.asrm.org/patients/factsheets/Older _Female-Fact.pdf

[6] Benjamin Spock's bible is:

> Spock, B. (1946) *The commonsense book of baby and childcare*, New York, NY: Simon and Schuster; 8th edn, 2004, Pocket Books.

[7] Penelope Leach's modern book is:

> Leach, P. (1979) *Baby and child*, London: Penguin.

[8] See Furedi, F. (2001) *Paranoid parenting*, London: Penguin.

[9] Larkin, P. (1971) 'This be the verse', published 1974 in *High Windows*, London: Faber and Faber.

[10] For a continuing claim that work and motherhood are incompatible see:

> de Marneffe, D. (2006) *Maternal desire*, London: Virago.

Chapter Ten

[1] Pugh, M. (2002) 'Working class experience and state social welfare 1908–1914: old age pensions reconsidered', *Historical Journal*, vol 45, pp 775-96.

[2] The most recent officially sponsored analysis of the policy options is:

> Turner, A. (2005) *Pensions in the UK*, London: HMSO.

[3] See Hill, M. (2007) *Pensions: Policy and politics in the twenty-first century*, Bristol: The Policy Press.

The government legislated to require all employers from 2012 to offer occupational pension schemes based on contributions of 4% of pay by the employer; 3% by the employee and 1% from the state, and with a specific requirement for those not willing to participate to opt out. This, however, is hardly likely to fill the gap for the lower paid and will result in large numbers of small savers. Their actual pension entitlements were made even more uncertain by the expectation that the private sector would have a major role in managing the funds and its record was one of charging typically 40% of funds entrusted to it for doing so. The new pensioners would be better off putting their money in National Savings or building society accounts.

[4] Age Concern (2006) 'Second class citizens in a first class country', *Reportage*, April, London: Age Concern.

See also:

Ginn, J. (2006) 'Spinning pensioner poverty figures', *Radical Statistics*, vol 88, pp 23–34.

Chapter Eleven

[1] Living wills are now governed by the Mental Capacity Act 2008.

[2] Debbie Purdy won her case in the House of Lords (see *Times Law Reports*, 31 July 2009), who enjoined the Director of Public Prosecutions to clarify policy on when those assisting suicide would be prosecuted. Interim policy guidelines were published on 23 September 2009, but did little more than clarify what was already evident. Those capable of making informed decisions could be helped by others to die provided the assister(s) did not stand to gain from the death. Those under 18 and those suffering from mental incapacity could not, legally, be assisted and every case is to be considered on its merits, so leaving many of those contemplating assisted suicide still in a quandary.

[3] Mary Warnock's quoted remarks are taken from *The Times*, 4 October 2008. See also:

Warnock, M. and Macdonald, E. (2008) *Easeful death: Is there a case for assisted dying?*, Oxford: Oxford University Press.

[4] *The Times*, 4 October 2008.

[5] Brown, G. (2008) *The living end: The future of death, aging and immortality*, Basingstoke: Palgrave.

[6] The Commission for Social Care Inspection, which inspected care homes, was superseded by the 'super-regulator' the Care Quality Commission in 2009. The CQC is responsible for all of the NHS, the local authorities and the private care sector. One advance is that homes run by the same company are registered as a group, rather than individually as before, so that failings can be remedied across the group and senior management held to account. Complaints about care are, however, devolved to the local government ombudsman, who has no specific expertise in the care of the elderly. Further, those opting to manage their own care and find specialist accommodation – so-called self-funders – were, in the proposals in 2008, left with no recourse for complaint. Residents risk being required to leave care homes if families pursue complaints with management. Self-funders who opt for making their own choices were hence in a very full sense expected to take responsibility for the consequences.

Chapter Twelve

[1] See:
   Durkheim, E. (1933) *The division of labour in free society*, New York, NY: The Free Press.
   Durkheim, E. (1952) *Suicide: A study in sociology*, London: RKP.
   Durkheim, E. (1957) *Professional ethics and civic morals*, London: RKP.

[2] Popper, K.R. (1963) *Conjectures and refutations*, London: Routledge.

Index

Note: Page numbers followed by *n* refer to information in a note.